£ 9.99

## Issues in Mental Health

*Series Editor*: Jo Campling

The care and status of persons with mental health problems has been identified as one of the key issues in health and society in the 1990s.

This series of books has been commissioned to give a multidisciplinary perspective: legal, medical, psychiatric and social work aspects of mental health will be covered. There is also an international perspective: wherever possible, books will compare developments in a range of different countries.

PUBLISHED

Suman Fernando
*Mental Health, Race and Culture*

Shulamit Ramon (editor)
*Beyond Community Care: Normalisation and Integration Work*

FORTHCOMING

Philip Bean and Patricia Mounser
*The Discharge of Psychiatric Patients*

Chris Heginbotham
*Mental Health and Human Rights*

Tessa Jowell and Gerald Wistow
*Community Care and Mental Health*

Ron Lacey, David Pilgrim and Anne Rogers
*People First: How Patients Experience Mental Health Care*

The *Issues in Mental Health* series is published in association with:

MIND (National Association for Mental Health)
22 Harley Street, London W1N 2ED (071–637–0741)

MIND is the leading mental health organisation in England and Wales. It works for a better life for people diagnosed, labelled or treated as mentally ill. It does this through campaigning, influencing government policy, training, education and service provision. Throughout its work MIND reflects its awareness of black and ethnic communities, and draws on the expertise of people with direct experience as providers and users of mental health services.

The points of view expressed in this publication do not necessarily reflect MIND policy.

# Beyond Community Care

## Normalisation and Integration Work

Edited by
**Shulamit Ramon**

in association
with

First published 1991

Published by
MACMILLAN EDUCATION LTD
Houndmills, Basingstoke, Hampshire RG21 2XS
and London
Companies and representatives
throughout the world

Edited and typeset by Povey/Edmondson
Okehampton and Rochdale, England

Printed in Hong Kong

British Library Cataloguing in Publication Data
Beyond community care: normalisation and integration work.
— (Issues in mental health)
1. Great Britain. Mentally ill persons. Rehabilitation
I. Ramon, Shulamit   II. Series
362.204250941
ISBN 0–333–51400–9 (hardcover)
ISBN 0–333–51401–7 (paperback)

---

**Series Standing Order   (Issues in Mental Health)**

If you would like to receive future titles in this series as they are
published, you can make use of our standing order facility. To place a
standing order please contact your bookseller or, in case of difficulty,
write to us at the address below with your name and address and the
name of the series. Please state with which title you wish to begin your
standing order. (If you live outside the United Kingdom we may not
have the rights for your area, in which case we will forward your order
to the publisher concerned.)

Standing Order Service, Macmillan Distribution Ltd,
Houndmills, Basingstoke, Hampshire, RG21 2XS, England

---

'But nobody wounded like him could deserve a chance at life. Better dead said the crones, better dead said history, better jump in at the deep end decided her strong soul as she heard his crest fallen cry. His mother it was who treated him as normal, tumbled to his intelligence, tumbled to his eye-signalled talk, tumbled to the hollyberries, green yet, but holding promise of burning in red given time, given home.'

Christopher Nolan, *Under the Eye of the Clock*.

To all of the discovered, and those yet to be discovered, Christopher Nolans of this world, their mothers, fathers, sisters and brothers.

# Contents

# List of Contributors

**David Brandon** is a social worker by training, formerly director of North-West Mind, editor of *Community Living*, author of several books, and currently training service providers in the field of learning difficulties. His most recent book is on brokerage.

**Mike Lawson** is the director of International Self-Advocacy Alliance, vice-chairperson of MIND, active in Survivors Speak Out, who has personally experienced the pyschiatric services as a recipient. He is involved in training and promoting self-advocacy and mutual support among users.

**Alexandra Lewis** is the chair of the British Community Health Councils organisation, and until recently also a member of the Mental Health Act Commission. She is a researcher and planner in the fields of developmental handicap and psychiatric services for offenders.

**Shulamit Ramon** is a social worker and clinical psychologist by training, senior lecturer at the London School of Economics, with a wide-ranging cross-national research background. She is the author of *Psychiatry in Britain: Meaning and Policy*, and the editor of *Psychiatry in Transition: British and Italian Experiences*.

**Julia Segal** is currently psychologist and researcher with ARMS (Action Research Multiple Sclerosis), author of *Fantasy in Everyday Life*, with considerable experience of work and training in different settings.

**Richard Warner** is the director of Boulder Mental Health Center, a large and innovative service. He is also professor of psychiatry at the University of Colorado and the author of *Recovery from Schizophrenia*.

# Acknowledgements

I would like to thank the contributors to this volume who gave freely of their creativity to the project, making my task as the editor rewarding.

As usual, Teodor helped with insightful and precise comments, while Aelita reminded me that there is an ordinary life to be lived and enjoyed; I am grateful to both of them. Lindsey Olliver helped in the typing with care and efficiency.

SHULAMIT RAMON

# Preface

The title of this book suggests that *community care*, a principle and a concept which dominated the approach to people with disabilities for the last thirty years throughout the Western world, has perhaps outlived its usefulness.

Developing during the Second World War and especially during the 1950s and 1960s, community care was a professional and political response to the guilt evoked by the restricted life led by people with disabilities in total institutions.[1] The ideal of desegregation resembled the achievement of the great age of reform which took place 200 years earlier, symbolised in freeing the residents of psychiatric hospitals from their chains by Pinel and Tuke. Furthermore, it was believed that by locating services outside the segregating institution, the need to enter it would decrease and integration with the ordinary community would take place spontaneously.

Thus community care included the recognition that many of the people with disabilities residing in institutions had the potential to lead a more ordinary life in the community. However, neither this recognition nor the ideal seems to have led to a fundamental change in social and professional approaches to people with disabilities.[2]

The focus on dehospitalisation — which constituted the bulk of community care efforts in the field of disability — as a once and for all solution to the problem was particularly attractive to politicians. They could easily identify with this simple humanistic message, made doubly attractive by the possibility of reducing public expenditure through care in the community.[3] With hindsight and the evidence accumulated since the 1950s, it seems that concentrating on the point of transfer has become a crucial stumbling block of the policy.[4] For it meant neglecting the process of change in the institution, its residents and workers prior to the move; paying little attention to the life led after leaving the institution; and even less attention to preventing the need for institutional life in the first place.

Community care has been bedevilled by a conceptual muddle, a policy muddle, and a practice muddle.

Conceptually, a community can be a neighbourhood, a community of interest with and without geographical boundaries, or the configuration of a person's connections and ties.[5] Care is about attending to people's needs in different ways, and at different levels, including unpaid and paid care, physical, financial and emotional care, *in* and *by* the community.[6] The lack of criteria for inclusion and exclusion among all these possibilities and for a qualitative range, inevitably leads to a muddle.

Perhaps because the concept was allowed to mean anything vaguely related to life outside a long-term institution, including contradictory meanings, it became more easily open to abuse at the policy level. Dehospitalisation, deinstitutionalisation and primarily the relocation of people into smaller units have become the hallmarks of the policy thrust. These three objectives differ in principle, and the lack of differentiation has led to undifferentiated policies. This state of affairs also enabled politicians to get away with a high degree of rhetoric and a considerably lower degree of financial and attitudinal commitment for most of the time.

The combination of a lack of clarity in concept and policy has inevitably led to a similar confusion and lack of differentiation at the level of implementation, of which there are numerous examples.

This state of affairs raises the question as to whether community care was ever given the proper conditions in which to be implemented,[7] or whether the flaws are too fundamental for it to be resurrected even if such conditions were to become available. This book focuses on the development of the related, but new and divergent approach of *normalisation, social role valorisation* and *integration* of people with disabilities. Leaving aside the unsuccessful aspects of community care, the new approach puts the emphasis on the quality of life of people with disabilities and on a change in attitudes and practices by all of us.

The failure of community care to live up to its promise makes the validity and claims of any alternative approach much riskier than they would have been. It also makes many of those previously involved in the community care endeavour wary of any new developments, and reaffirms those who never accepted it in the righteousness of their belief. Therefore, the reception of a new framework which starts from where community care ended is bound to be sceptical at best.

In this book we attempt to examine whether the moral, conceptual and practical implications of the framework offered around the principles of normalisation, social role valorisation, and integration could constitute a suitable replacement for that of community care, and to investigate the limitations and contradictions of the new approach.

Focusing on these three key principles, and the practices related to them, the text investigates their meanings and implications across the range of physical disability, learning difficulties and mental distress in the First World. This is not to suggest that they are irrelevant in the Second and Third Worlds, or to imply that the First World has nothing to learn in the field of disability from the other two. The focus on the First World is aimed at locating the new direction within the cultural and structural context in which it has developed. This new framework has evolved since the late 1950s; moving from the Scandinavian countries to North America and from there to the rest of Europe, including Britain. It was connected with a parallel, interrelated development in Italy, yet one with a distinct character of its own. The cultural map of this newly charted route is fascinating in the light it sheds not only on when and where social innovations come into being, but how and why, what stands on their way, and what promotes them.

The right of those with disabilities to an ordinary life, and its implementation, presents a challenge to us all because it entails a view of people with disabilities as people first and disabled second. This emphasis focuses on their abilities and not just on the disabilities, on their equality as citizens, their right to social support, as well as their duty to contribute to communal life according to ability.

Furthermore, the definition of 'ability' is considerably broadened within this new approach, to include everyday qualities which do not depend on competition and exploitation but on giving and taking at the social and emotional levels, as well as at the performance and intellectual levels.[8] In the light of this focus, most of our cherished beliefs about people with disabilities, typified by a condescending and distancing attitude, are questioned.

The new framework challenges:

1. The general public who in the main has often discriminated negatively against people with disabilities, or at best treated them with indifference.
2. The politicians and mass media, both attempting to represent and to shape public opinion.
3. Accepted professional attitudinal, conceptual and practice paradigms.
4. The informal carers of people with disabilities who were often let down and isolated by others, who have campaigned on behalf of people with disabilities in contradictory directions, and who are now campaigning more and more on their own behalf.
5. The self-image and self-approach of people with disabilities.

A number of different constituents are therefore inherently involved in the normalisation project: people with disabilities, their families and close friends, professional service providers, policy-makers, politicians, the media, ordinary people without an identified disability, and the groups which represent them. This book is addressed to all of these as it outlines their concerns and explores their potential and actual contribution to the project.

The first part of the book investigates the values and conceptual knowledge bases, as well as that of skills. In view of the lack of conceptual clarity surrounding the principle of community care, it is important to know what is meant by the different concepts and whether their meanings are compatible. It is equally important to ascertain if in fact they add something new to our knowledge and practice which was not there previously; whether they omit that which needs to be understood in relation to disability, people who suffer from it, their context and the service context. The first part also looks at issues as to whether the new framework simply denies the existence of a disability, or asks people with disabilities to become superhuman. It is central to know as well whether the knowledge and the objectives are closely related before the issue of implementation is considered. Part I begins with what has already been built up since the late 1950s, some of which has attained the status of 'classics', and examines this body of knowledge respectfully but irreverently. The development of the principles of normalisation and social role valorisation (SRV) owes a lot to Wolf Wolfensberger.[9] By now there are additional and somewhat different frameworks on normalisation, such as that offered by John O'Brien and Alan Tyne,[10] of which account is taken in this book.

Furthermore, the commitment to a critical examination of the approach implies an analysis which exposes its weaknesses too, as well as original additions to some elements of the SRV approach. The latter are not limited to the first part of the book. They include the analysis of the actual responses of professionals in the field of disability – those which are not to be found in the textbooks – and their implications for normalisation work (Chapters 2,3,4); the place of recipients of services in rethinking and changing the service system (Chapters 2,3,4,5); the analysis of obstacles to citizen participation (Chapter 6); the creative use of available resources in building new programmes which follow intergration principles (Chapters 2,3,5,7); and the application of knowledge from anthropology, sociology, social administration, social psychology (Chapters 1,4,6,7) together with users' experiential knowledge of issues such as changing professional and personal attitudes (included in each chapter). The implementation of the objectives of normalisation demands a radical change in the current approach to people with disabilities and to the services available to them. For that to happen, attitudes, concepts, policies and strategies would have to change too. The enormity of the task means that bringing together all these components is a precondition to a significant move towards a genuine effort to implement these goals.

The different participants of the social role valorisation task are represented and looked at in particular in the second part of the book, by contributors who include the direct users of the services (namely people who are defined as having a disability), the professionals, the managers of services who are responsible for making a reality out of global policy directives, and the representatives of the general public in this process. In a way, they are all asking and attempting to answer the question as to whether it is realistically possible to implement the objectives of normalisation, social role valorisation and integration.

The third and final part provides an overview of the development of policies with which to implement SRV principles. It capitalises on the insight and examples provided in the other chapters, while offering additional illustrations and a more comprehensive perspective of policy issues.

The text describes and critically examines issues at the personal and the social levels, macro and micro layers, the material and the symbolic facets of our lives. The authors do not shy away from indicating conflicts and ambiguities where these exist. A further enriching facet is offered by the inclusion of the cross-national and cross-cultural perspectives in the book, in evidence in each chapter. This is particularly important because so much of the opportunities for social role valorisation and integration depend on welfare structures and on the specific meanings attached to these principles. This perspective is aimed at enabling the reader to evaluate the advantages and disadvantages of the impact of different welfare strategies, as well as those of specific programmes and culturally determined attitudes. The availability of diverse approaches within the Western world presented in this volume, their advantages and disadvantages, should put to rest any simplistic notion of an overall superiority of one country over the other.

As already stated, it has been the aim to incorporate different types of disabilities in the examination of the normalisation framework. This is based on the belief that the values, concepts, and skills which underlie the framework are of equal relevance to the whole range of disabilities, due to the shared element of the social and personal response to disability and to people perceived as embodying it. The validity of this approach is evident in the exploration of issues such as professional distancing, citizen participation, empowering users, the common need for housing, income, employment, and friendship. Yet, taking this line is not without its problems, as is illustrated best in relation to mental illness/distress. This 'scandlising category' protrudes as the odd one out in a number of ways, ranging from the unresolved difficulties of defining it as a personal disability, attitudes towards the category and the people who personify it, the pace of implementing normalisation policies, to the impatience of normalisation protagonists with the basic aetiological dilemmas related to mental distress, and with the professionals working in this field.

The collection is not intended as a DIY manual but as an exploration of the richness and complexity of the approach, which advocates the blending of theoretical and applied knowledge, attitudes with conceptual frameworks and a range of skills to match. The book does not offer an exhaustive coverage of all the evidence or of all that has been published in relation to the approach. The text, however, is comprehensive in providing an overview in Parts I and III and specific perspectives in Part II. In so doing, it offers simultaneously a broad canvas together with deeper, yet narrower, filters. It is up to the readers to decide what of the rich menu on offer would suit them best.

The contributors to this book come from a wide range of personal and professional experience; a necessity in meeting the challenge of exploring the complexity of the issues under discussion. As is evident in the text, the contributors do not necessarily agree on all issues, including some fundamental areas such as the value of existing professional expertise. Nevertheless, they all share the belief that people with disabilities have the right and the ability to enjoy a dignified and enriched life, provided they are given the right support. Each author attempts in his or her own way to take us further along the road to achieving this objective, via a knowledgeable and challenging route.

Writing at the beginning of the 1990s with an eye to the twenty first century, it is impossible to escape the sense of a cold welfare climate prevailing throughout the Western world.[11] This has meant cuts in public expenditure and in spending on welfare services; a greater focus on providing services seen to offer good value for money from the point of view of some, which is perceived by others as trying to provide a service on the cheap, based on exploitation of a large number of ordinary citizens; and attempts to cut down considerably on the responsibility of the collective towards its more vulnerable members.

Perhaps in response to this coldness we have also witnessed an upsurge in innovation in the fields of welfare and services for people with disabilities. This covers aspects such as new conceptual development and a more critical approach to conceptualisation, new organisational structures, new entrepreneurs such as the users of the services themselves, and a better quality of service and life resulting from these changes, in many instances.

For between the cold climate and the clients stand people – professionals, informal carers, users, some politicians, a few journalists, or just responsible citizens – loyal to the cause of improving the lot of those with disabilities and who have responded with a greater effort than ever before.

The book is a testimonial to this innovative upsurge, which hopefully will sustain all those involved and interested in the field of disability during the inevitable tribulations of the next decade and beyond.

## References

1. Deutsch, A., *The Shame of the States* (New York: Harcourt, Brace, 1948).
2. Ramon, S., *Psychiatry in Britain: Meaning and Policy* (London: Croom Helm, 1985).
3. Scull, A., *Decarceration – Community Treatment and the Deviant: A Radical View* (Englewood Cliffs, NJ: Prentice-Hall, 1977).
4. Brown, P., *The Transfer of Care* (London: Routledge & Kegan Paul, 1985).
5. McGee, J., *Gentle Teaching: A Non-aversive Approach to Helping Persons with Mental Retardation* (Nebraska: Human Sciences Press, 1987).
6. Bulmer, M., *The Social Base of Community Care* (London: Allen & Unwin, 1987).
7. Finch, J. and Groves, D. (eds), *A Labour of Love* (London: Routledge & Kegan Paul, 1984).
8. Malin, N. (ed.), *Community Care Reassessed* (London, Croom Helm, 1987).
9. Wolfensberger, W., *The Principle of Normalisation in Human Services*, (Toronto: National Institute on Mental Retardation, 1972); Wolfensberger, W., 'Social Role Valorisation: A Proposed New Term for the Principle of Normalisation', *Mental Retardation*, vol. 21, no. 6, December 1983, pp. 234–9.

10. O'Brien, J. and Tyne, A., *The Principle of Normalisation: A Foundation for Effective Services* (London: CMHERA, 1981).
11. Glennerster, H. (ed.), *Welfare in a Cold Climate* (London: Heinemann, 1983).

# Part I
# The Background Dimensions of Normalisation Work

# Introduction

This part of the book looks closely at the major concepts, values, theoretical knowledge, skills and attitudes entailed in the development of the new approach, each feeding back into the high level of interrelatedness which exists among all these components.

One of the hallmarks of the approach which has been followed throughout the text is the attention paid to the issue as to whether language, attitudes, behaviour and structures meet the values which they are meant to represent. This focus on ethics stands out against the background of the current priority given to the scientific status of clinical work in medicine and psychology over ethical considerations, and the denial of the relevance of these issues in disciplines such as economics. The equal attention paid to the material and the symbolic facets in the lives of people with disability is another expression of the comprehensiveness of the social role valorisation approach.

Readers anxious to get into 'the real world' of practice are invited not only to contain their suspense, but to modify their view of the world to one which recognises the importance of understanding its roots in values and conceptual thinking, not less than in practice wisdom.

Furthermore, the emphasis in Chapter 1 on looking at the interrelations between values and knowledge, and in Chapter 2 on skills and values, traditional and newly developed professional wisdom, is aimed at encouraging readers to put their critical faculties to use no less than their abilities to absorb new ideas.

It is only by linking the different dimensions in Chapters 1 and 2 that the complexity of the new approach comes to the fore, that its internal contradictions become clearer, and that its contribution can began to be assessed.

Each of the two chapters focuses on what is distinctly innovative in the approach, and where it is challenging accepted norms, beliefs and vested interests. Knowledge from different disciplines and relevant experiential knowledge is outlined, together with the areas where knowledge is still missing. In so doing, both authors 'deviate' considerably from what has become the new 'orthodoxy' of the normalisation approach.

Brandon proposes what should be shed as compared with what should be added to the existing skills of welfare professionals, while posing the challenge of emergent new groups of providers and the empowering of users of the established professions. He has chosen a personalised style which fits his message well and offers personal examples regarding its implications, as well as the difficulties and the rewards entailed within it. Using a more academic style, Ramon looks at the potential contribution of developing a truly multidisciplinary knowledge base to serve the new approach. She explores the different and somewhat contradictory motivations behind the adoption of normalisation principles. In particular she focuses on the processes of change in relation to professionals and to organisational innovation.

The investigation of these two themes is taken up from a different angle by Brandon when he looks at the management skills required for normalisation work.

While providing an overview, the two chapters demonstrate the integration and interrelationships between theory and practice which is the hallmark of this book. Brandon's call for *practical dreamers* is echoed here at the theoretician's level no less than at the practitioner's, and throughout the book at all other levels of participation in the normalisation process.

'In 1940, two grey buses with windows painted grey drove up to the institution for the first of many trips. The driver presented a list of residents who were to be "transferred" and then drove them off after saying to the worker "soon there will be seventy-five less idiots in the world".

Karl fought with the driver and ran away shouting "I'll hang myself before I'll die like that." Richard, who was paralyzed, knew he did not have a chance; with calm and purpose he gave his pocket money and watch to his closest friend. He discussed the situation with his housefather, and they prayed together as he made himself ready to die like a man with dignity.'

R. Perske, 'The Dignity of Risk', in W. Wolfensberger (ed.), *The Principle of Normalisation in Human Services*

# 1
# Principles and Conceptual Knowledge
*Shulamit Ramon*

Normalisation is defined as the principle by which people with a disability have the right to lead a valued ordinary life, based on the belief in their equality as human beings and citizens.

Nirje perceived normalisation as

> making available [to the mentally retarded] patterns and conditions of everyday life which are as close as possible to the norms and patterns of the mainstream of society. An ordinary life includes a normal rhythm of days, weeks and years, normal-sized living units, adequate privacy, normal access to social, emotional and sexual relationships with others, normal growing-up experiences, the possibility of decently paid work, choice and participation in decisions affecting one's future.[1]

This list includes features which are taken for granted by people without a disability, usually unaware that they are absent from the lives of many people with a disability.

In 1983, Wolfensberger proposed that the term normalisation be replaced by that of social role valorisation (SRV).[2] He believes that positive social revaluation of people with a disability will be achieved by their performance of socially desirable roles and through being treated as valued people by society. From the outset normalisation is presented as a value preference, illustrating the strong moral strand embedded in the approach.

By definition the approach applies to every type of disability and the people who suffer from it, ranging from physical disability, through developmental disability, to mental distress. This is justified by the assumption that they all share the impact which social attitudes to disability have on leading an ordinary life. The loss due to the disability *per se* is hardly focused upon in the literature on normalisation.

What is an ordinary life? Nirje's description focuses on opportunities for ordinary living but does not offer a definition of it. Being members of a particular society and class we are all aware of the variations in lifestyle of different groups, to the point that the intuitive reaction to the concept of 'an ordinary life' is to deny that it exists. Yet when we compare those variations with the life led by the majority of people with a recognised disability in our society, it is

6

possible to pinpoint the differences. These include an inferior degree of control over their lives, choice, richness of stimuli and social encounters, starting with simply being poor. Furthermore, it has been suggested that to aspire to an ordinary life for people with a disability is to wish on them pettiness, conformity and boredom.[3] While this is a tempting suggestion, it disregards the past and present social position of people with a disability. This is typified by either being unable and/or not allowed to choose whether to be conforming and bored or to be non-conforming and creative, a choice which is open to people without a disability, albeit within limits.

Without necessarily glorifying the quality of ordinary living, it is unashamedly assumed within the normalisation approach that such a lifestyle is qualitatively better than the one currently available to most people with a disability in Western societies. A separate, yet related issue is whether the approach has an inherent preference for a middle-class, Christian (but not Calvinist), Western lifestyle, in particular North American and Northern European. The emphasis in the literature has been not only on the individual but also on highly individualised, non-competitive lifestyles and services, a clear preference for services outside the public sector, and a noticeable lack of interest in collective existence. For example, in some cases there is stress on mutual support or citizen-advocacy, but not on solidarity. However, the focus on a non-competitive lifestyle differs considerably from the present ethos of the middle classes in North America and Northern Europe. Thus an ambigiuity is retained as to the ideal type of lifestyle on which the SRV approach is based.

## 1 Unpacking the definition

### 1.1 Deinstitutionalisation

SRV protagonists have been unanimous in campaigning against placing people with disabilities in institutions, and for enabling those who live in such establishments to leave. Underlying this preference is the belief that institutional existence is an anathema to ordinary living, and that it is crucial to prevent the institutionalisation of new facilities which are actually created outside the old institutions. Therefore, understanding the significance of institutional life, and of dismantling it, is central to understanding the approach.

The history of creating institutions for people with disabilities is full of good intentions and improvements in living conditions. It also served to segregate them further from the rest of the population, making them wholly dependent on the institution, without privacy and choice.[4] The function of caring for this group was interwoven with that of social control and isolation. In turn, the isolation heightened the impression that they were a race apart and hence reinforced the stigma attached to them.

Wing coined the term *'institutionalism'* at the beginning of the 1960s.[5] Writing about psychiatric patients, he saw mental distress as the primary source of the social disability which so many of the residents exhibited. The passive, regimented lifestyle in the hospital was perceived as leading to secondary impairments in terms of deficiency in social and self-care skills.

Barton,[6] in his pamphlet entitled *Institutional Neurosis* (published in 1959), proposed that the structure of psychiatric hospitals induces a neurosis-like state for both patients and staff.

Goffman's *'total institution'*[7] differs from these two perspectives in a number of ways. Living in such an institution is portrayed by him as a life apart from the rest of humanity, in which people are stripped of dignity, privacy, choice and control, in return for shelter and some forms of professional intervention. Although not meant as a punishment for people with disabilities – unlike those in prison – the similarity with a prison regime as portrayed by him is uncanny.

The analysis of institutions provided by Goffman, Foucault and Basaglia[8] suggests that it is the structural nature of these establishments which leads to the oppressing of residents and staff alike, rather than the 'badness' of the staff or the administration. Basaglia in particular argued that it is the social control function of total institution which cannot but result in oppression.[9]

While the normalisation approach echoes the influence of both institutionalism (in not denying the existence of a disability and its possible impact) and total institutions, it follows Goffman's analysis more closely.

However, the approach has gone further than both Goffman and Basaglia in attempting to prevent the institutionalisation of services and residential settings outside the hospital. In so doing, a clear disagreement is expressed with the prevalent belief of professionals and politicians in the First World, that basing services outside total institutions and in small localities is a sufficient condition to ensure the lack of institutionalisation. The concept is used within the approach to signify structural features of a service which may induce institutionalism and alternatives to them, rather than as a description of qualities of individual users, as suggested by Wing.[10]

To date the issue of how to dismantle an institution is yet to be addressed by SRV protagonists. This serious omission may be linked to the strong emphasis on individuals rather than on the collective, to not taking organisational issues seriously, and the disinterest in the issue of social control. Only Psichiatria Democratica (the Italian reform movement) has attempted to provide an analytical framework for the processes involved in this thorny issue, which it put into practice in the good examples of the Italian psychiatric reform.[11] The main components of such a major structural change will be outlined in Chapter 7.

## 1.2 Social role valorisation

Most people depend for their self-perception and social standing on how they are valued socially. Each society has roles, settings, behaviours and emotions which it values more than others, and those which are devalued. Positive and negative social sanctions are attached to valued and devalued social behaviour respectively.

In applying these basic sociological concepts to the normalisation approach, it is suggested that the following process is taking place:

(a) people with a disability are perceived as being different in a negative sense;
(b) this has led in the last two centuries to their segregation from ordinary people and ordinary living patterns;
(c) the segregation has meant that the majority of people with a disability have been prevented from performing socially valued roles and behaviours to a large extent;
(d) consequently, they have been further devalued.

Thus a double act of devaluation has taken place; one at the beginning of the process and one at its end, with ordinary people being socialised not to recognise that the second is largely the outcome of the first, and genuinely believing that people with disabilities cannot assume socially valued roles because of the disability.

Devaluation takes many forms: rejection, distantiation, segregation, congregation, discontinuity, loss of autonomy, deindividualisation, disenfranchisement, dependency on artificial, paid relationships, involuntary systematised proverty, being suspected of multiple problems, being negatively imaged, brutalisation and awareness of oneself as devalued and as a burden to others.[12]

A crucial component of leading an ordinary life lies in behaving in a socially valued way and in being positively valued by others.

Logically, it would be assumed that the first leads to the second, but the awareness of existing feedback relationships between these two elements is a central conceptual and practice issue within the SRV approach. Psychology teaches us that people improve their level of functioning and self-image often because of the encouragement offered by others, and because of the close relationships between self and others' expectations. This makes even more sense in the case of those who have developed a low self-image resulting from being socially devalued, as so many people with a disability have experienced. Therefore, SRV can become a meaningful process only if it is reciprocal.

The literature on SRV accepts the necessity to cater for the culturally relative definitions of what is and what is not socially valued.[13] This indicates an acceptance of pluralism within one society. Yet this is to duck the issue of cultural hegemony and to deny that in each society there is a discontinuous scale in which the valued is sharply differentiated from the devalued. This dichotomous range serves the purpose of social control, making the understanding of both cultural hegemony and social control mechanisms indispensable for the normalisation approach.[14] An extreme example of the effect of escaping from cultural hegemony and social control was provided by people living in Nazi Germany, who actively opposed the regime and became socially devalued within their own society, to the point of risking their lives.

Therefore, there is a price to be paid for being considered socially valued and there is a need to work constantly on expanding the range of what is considered to be so, if people with disabilities are to be allowed to become genuine partners. An uncomfortable example is provided by the emphasis within the SRV approach on the right of people with a disability to sexual enjoyment, including those who need the physical help of others in achieving it.[15]

Within the SRV approach it becomes necessary to ask whether people are behaving according to their age and gender, and whether they are given the opportunity and support required for it to take place. This includes the liberating realisation that adults in many Western societies live on their own, and not with their parents. Therefore, people with a disability do not have to live with their parents to conform with the norm. Yet class, gender and ethnicity have not received the same attention within the SRV approach, perhaps because they are more divisive than unifying factors, and go against the grain of the underlying hegemony of middle-class standards within the approach.

The emphasis on everyday life has led to the recognition that many socially valued roles are not based on a competitive effort. Being a friend, a daughter or son, a grandchild, a grandparent, a parent, a neighbour, a consumer — are all relevant examples of the type of roles which are no less the backbone of our societies than those based on competition. However, this view overlooks the fact that the most powerful roles in our societies relate to adult working and political life, in which competition is rife.

Should social role valorisation replace normalisation as the name of the approach? SRV is less overtly conforming to the statistical and largely mythical majority. Unlike normalisation, it has not been a term used previously by conquerors in speaking about the conquered, and it is conceptually more precise. However, SRV denotes an overemphasis on roles as the backbone of social existence, and is even less familiar and less intuitively understood than normalisation is to lay and professional people.

### 1.3 Opportunities for ordinary living

These form the crucial background to adopting socially valued roles, to the possibility of moving out of an institution and of leading a non-institutionalised life.

The opportunities should cover the major areas of everyday life, such as income, housing, work, education, health services, recreation, and social interaction. Support services should be available as much as possible within the range of universally available communal services, rather than as singled out, ghettoised services. This does raise the issue of the desirability of any specialist facility.

One of the best examples in which such an opportunity is provided is in the integrated education of children with special needs in ordinary schools, currently adopted in a number of Western countries, with Denmark, Italy and Norway in the lead.[16] These experiences have demonstrated that it is possible and desirable to do so, from the perspective of the social interaction of those with and without a disability, and that it can be achieved with very little parental or teacher opposition.

### 1.4 The meaning of the disability

An approach which focuses so much on people with a disability needs to clarify the meaning of disability for the person and his/her society. Surprisingly, this is not the case. In most of the literature, the disability is put aside as a factor which limits the person in one way or another, and which may therefore require an effort to sort it out in order to get on with ordinary living.[17] 'Sorting out' may also imply accepting the limitation as a given which cannot be changed, in the same way that most of us accept that we lack a specific talent or skill, and that there is nothing we can do about it. This reflects the view of disability as part of everyone's socially acceptable imperfection. Yet another possibility, expressed in a minority of the literature,[18] is to see oneself as positively special because of having to live with the disability and becoming a better person than the average as a result of this struggle. Finally, there is the view that what matters is the dignity of one's life, and that when life is measured by the degree of dignity the disability is meaningless.[19]

On the whole, most of the protagonists of the SRV approach do not deny that the disability does matter, creates an additional burden and does not automatically make people into better persons. Thus in principle there is no glorification of disability, unlike the claim by the anti-psychiatry movement in the 1960s that people with mental distress are 'special' in terms of being more soul-searching and less ready to conform socially.[20] The comparison with the anti-psychiatry approach is of particular interest because both utilise greatly the labelling school of deviancy (see section 3.1).

However, the issue of the emotional acceptance of the disability and the sense of loss felt by the person with a disability (and those close to him/her) is usually ignored by the protagonists of the SRV approach, perhaps because of the focus on leading an ordinary life. Segal, in Chapter 4, illustrates how important this issue is for the person and for the service providers. Accepting mental distress as a disability presents an even more complex issue than that of accepting either a physical or a mental handicap. Such an acceptance implies that the propensity of suffering from mental distress remains with the person for a long time and has to be taken into account as a background vulnerability. The latter is a claim which many of those active in the mental health users movement would be unhappy with (see Chapter 3).

## 2    The underlying values

It has become fashionable to express disdain at 'value talk',[21] seen as talk without substance. Thus David Brandon is poking fun at it in Chapter 2, while decrying the relative lack of 'skill talk' in the normalisation approach. Value talk is open to abuse when it remains only at the preaching level. Endorsing Wolfensberger's belief in the power of ideologies to shape our lives,[22] I see it as necessary to state explicitly what the SRV approach stands for.

Values are important as guidelines both to our interpretation of reality and our attempts to change it. The more taken for granted a value is, the more powerful it becomes in terms of its hold over our views and actions because it is less open for reconsideration.

### 2.1 People First

The most fundamental value of the normalisation approach is the belief that despite their problems, the people with a disability are first and foremost people just like those without.[23] This may sound simplistic, but the image conjured by terms such as 'the mentally handicapped' or 'the chronically mentally ill' as walking disabilities deserves to be corrected.

Within the approach the focus is on how much alike people with and without a disability really are. Being alike extends beyond the present into the future, in terms of having the potential to become more similar in performance and value.

This strong belief is another demarcating line between the traditional professional and lay approaches to those with a disability and the normalisation protagonists. It is about accrediting these individuals with dignity and rights even if they cannot attain the level of performance reached by those without a disability.

It is from this core value that the right of all of us to be supported by society at times of need stems. This is not due to potential productivity but to the human qualities and the potential for enriching our non-material life which people with a disability have in common with others.

The belief in the common humanity of all of us is also at the root of the modern concept of citizenship and the principle of equity in law enshrined in the constitutions of Western societies. In practice, this is not always the case even now. For example, British people with disabilities who reside in institutions are still facing obstacles which prevent many of them from voting (see the description of the study by Dyer in Chapter 2).

### 2.2 Respect for persons

This value follows directly from the belief in the personhood of people with a disability. It is also related to the concept of SRV because the demonstration of respect is one of the sanctions attached to socially valued people. Furthermore, it enables us to establish the principle by which a good service is one which you, a self-respecting and socially valued individual, would like to use too.

There are many forms which respect for people takes; some are more difficult to maintain in certain situations. For example, when adults are unable to look after their own basic bodily functions and depend on others for that, or when elderly people become confused, it seems 'natural' to treat them as babies. Yet some of us are able to continue to treat these people according to their age, rather than their degree of dependency.

Another form of respect has recently been highlighted by O'Brien.[24] He advises against using pain as part of the range of professional methods, not even in the case of challenging behaviour, and demonstrates the effectiveness of methods which utilise reward or ignoring strategies.

### 2.3    *The right to self-determination*

This value relates to the first two. It accords people the right to decide for themselves, based on their capability to reach sensible decisions and to have more in-depth knowledge about themselves than others would possess. These assumptions clash with the popular belief that professionals know better and with the possibility that many people who led either a segregated or an isolated life are unlikely to be sufficiently well informed and able to judge – two necessary qualities for good decision-making. The normalisation approach gets by these doubts by treating professional knowledge as a layer of information which should be made available to the person in an understandable language, and by proposing that decision-making be taught. The pamphlet *Officer Handbook*, produced by the People First project, illustrates how the skills for group decision-making can be introduced with humour and in a down to earth fashion to people long used to being the subject of others' decisions.[25]

In reality, the right to choose includes the right to make mistakes. Usually, most of us are afraid of failure and would opt for the least risky choice, however boring and unrewarding it may be. People with a disability are no exception to this commonsensical observation, especially those who have lived without any real say for many years. Therefore, when the protagonists of maintaining institutions suggest that many users would like to stay there, this could be the case. However, the other camp would argue – and offer ample evidence – that when informed of the choice of living outside in a non-threatening and meaningful way, most of the residents would opt to move out.[26] Furthermore, in line with the right to self-determination, those who opt to stay there after becoming informed and skilled in decision-making should be allowed to do so. This may create havoc in terms of large-scale planning, but the approach has been consistently to advocate small-scale, tailor-made planning in preference to the large-scale type, so liked by bureaucrats.

More risky choices are usually those about which users and workers may disagree, and may also be the more creative options. Given the investment in success and in the professional power to make decisions, it is not surprising that the notion of the right to fail is missing from the vocabulary of most helping professions. It is to be found in social work literature, the one profession more preoccupied with values than most others. Soyer[27] writes that the fears of the worker may be well justified, but above all they represent his/her fear of failure because going along with the users' choice implies sharing in the risk. The examples which Soyer provides are all taken from the field of physical disability and relate to the areas of work and education. They demonstrate that a number of clients succeeded where failure was predicted by their worker, despite, or in spite of, this being given as a powerful message to people whose self-confidence is often low.

The lesson which he emphasises is that in most cases it might be advisable to support a client in attempting to achieve an option which the worker deems as unobtainable. Since regardless of success or failure, very important principles would be established in such a case, namely, the right of the client to self-determination and the readiness of the worker to respect the choice, enabling the two of them to work better together in the future. You may rebel against this assertion by proposing that the price paid for this learning is too high in the case of failure. This may be true in some extreme situations, such as the client being abused or abusing others as the result of the choice. However, short of imminent danger to oneself and others, most other failures can be turned into positive learning experiences if the client feels that the worker respects the choice, despite disagreeing with it. Most of us learn through our mistakes, and to protect people with disabilities from making mistakes is unrealistic and patronising. Workers have the duty to ensure that clients are aware of the disadvantages and risks embedded in their choices, but not to make the decision instead of the users in most instances. While the protagonists of the normalisation approach seem to be unaware of the term 'the right to fail', several of them have suggested that risk-taking by service providers is a necessary step on the road which enables users to take responsibility and enjoy a greater degree of autonomy. Perske's 'dignity of risk'[28] emphasises the ability of people with disabilities to take moral and altruistic decisions in risky situations. Deinstitutionalisation too often calls for risk-taking; the first few times in which psychiatric patients became visible in their own communities included funny and hair-raising moments in the Italian experiences.[29]

Self-determination is always exercised within social boundaries, a feature accepted within the SRV approach as part of social life. Hence the focus on it is more of a plea for pluralism and flexibility in choices, instead of castigating people who opt for the less popular options into the role of deviants.

### 2.4   Is there a right to be dependent? The relationship between dependency and autonomy

On the face of it, our society has a clear-cut negative stance concerning dependency. Being independent is prescribed as the ideal, with dependency being portrayed as a personal weakness and a failure. At the same time, a large number of people without any disability are encouraged to remain dependent for longer and longer periods, such as young people, mothers and wives. Their dependency lies at the financial, social position and social network levels. While little is said about the fostered dependency of these groups, attempts by group members to become autonomous are portrayed as 'rebellious', 'premature', and 'irresponsible'. At the same time the dependency of working men on their partners and on their children at the emotional and practical levels is rarely made explicit. Thus the inevitable interdependency of each of us is being treated in a highly contradictory manner. People with a disability are expected to become more dependent on informal carers and service providers than they were before having the disability. In fact the term 'patient' says it all. To be a good patient is to become passive and dependent, not to express one's wishes, criticism or unhappiness. It is also about falling in with routines prescribed by others and having at best only a limited degree of control over one's life.

On the surface, the SRV approach calls for the adoption of autonomy and for discarding dependency. Yet the emphasis on the right to mutual and professional support implies the right to be dependent in certain conditions and times. The focus on the autonomy of people with disabilities, who are going to require the support of others, illustrates that implicit acceptance of inter-dependency as a positive state of being.

## 2.5 Empowerment

This is one of the latest catchphrases to be introduced in and out of the normalisation approach, to emphasise the need to give power to people with disabilities, and for them to take it and use it. The focus on this concept illustrates the awareness of the relative lack of power by most service users, especially those with an identified disability. For real empowerment to happen, power would have to be diverted from a number of groups, including professionals, informal carers, friends, central and local government, and voluntary activists. For power to be taken and used effectively by hitherto service recipients, they would need to come to terms not only with methods of using power but to be sufficiently self-assured as to their right to have it.

Freire[30] has demonstrated in his work with Brazilian peasants the power of knowledge (in this case of literacy) as a tool of empowerment. His work highlights the relationships between the stimuli for learning and the ability to overcome obstacles to learning by people who for long saw themselves as downtrodden, and were treated as such by others.

The five service accomplishments proposed by O'Brien[31] – presence, choice and autonomy, competence, status, and participa-tion – are the substance of what empowerment is about. For me empowerment is not an additional value, since it is adequately covered by that of self-determination when the latter is taken seriously.

The use of the concept of empowerment by politicians, who are constantly cutting back on services and benefits available to people with disabilities, does not merely ring hollow. It indicates the dangers inherent in confusing buying power with empowerment. While the availability of the first may enhance the second (see the discussion of brokerage in Chapter 2 and that of self-advocacy in Chapter 3), it is a travesty of empowerment to assume that it is no more than buying power, or that people without such a power have less right to empowerment. If any, within the normalisation approach, the latter have more of this right than those with buying power.

## 3   The knowledge base

The knowledge base is necessary for the understanding of the origins of the normalisation approach, its value base, and for its implementation. It could assist in highlighting contradictory and complementary elements, and in indicating the missing elements of knowledge. The content of such knowledge is the focus of this section.

### *The case for multifaceted knowledge*

Multifaceted knowledge is required to address the complexity of motivating people with a disability, the providers of services and the general public towards a considerable change in attitudes, skills, organisational structures, and opportunities for ordinary living. Psychology, sociology, anthropology, architecture, physiology, industrial relations, economics, history and philosophy are some of the disciplines contributing to this knowledge.

The approach has also been to reintroduce the subjective experiences of people with disabilities, preferably as told by them, as an integral and central source of knowledge. This follows from the belief that people's own knowledge of themselves is as valid as that of others (the additional value of this method is referred to in Chapters 2,3 and 4).

A further extension of this type of knowledge would be that of the providers' experiential understanding. Providers, especially professional ones, are usually encouraged not to express their emotions and to remain cool and detached. This is understandable given the wish for impartiality and the fear of breaking down under the stress of living at close quarters with the pain and suffering which people with disabilities endure at times. Yet the focus on the experiential aspect of this type of work could in fact relieve providers of some of the burden and enable them to share it with others, both colleagues and users. Greater use could also be made of providers' own experiences of suffering so that they become a source of knowledge as to what has been helpful and what has not, which component of the experience was the most bothersome, humiliating, informative or uplifting. Brandon (in Chapter 2) and Segal (in Chapter 4) provide examples of the usefulness of such an approach.

Systematic research of the clients' perspective, currently located mainly in anthropology, medical sociology and social work, has already been useful in understanding how they experience disability, being a service user, and different interventions.[32] Service users value being respected, being treated with honesty, and are aware of the sense of helplessness experienced by the professionals.

Poetry, biographies, novels and the theatre provide yet another source of knowledge which is rarely used in order to understand better the emotional level and the range of experiences which people with disabilities and those close to them may be going through.

Integrating all these diverse sources of knowledge into a coherent framework is necessary, but inevitably difficult. This is all the more complex because of the underlying ideologies with which each of these types of knowledge is endowed.

### 3.1 Understanding the processes of social devaluation and processes of revaluation

Social role valorisation is derived directly from the symbolic interactionism school within sociology and social psychology, influenced especially by the labelling approach to deviancy.[33] There it is argued that deviant acts or qualities, deemed socially as negatively valued and different from those expected normatively, may end in the actor being labelled by representatives of society as deviant. The approach is particularly weak in explaining who is more likely to be labelled as deviant when acting similarly, or in which circumstances labelling is more likely to happen. Instead, it has focused on the process of being labelled. The elements common to all types of deviancy include:

1. Assessing the person as the focus of the deviancy rather than attributing it to external factors (society, parents, peer group).
2. Generalising from one act or one quality to the totality of the person.
3. Re-evaluating the person's past in the light of the present.
4. Attributing a prognosis in which the future is predicted.

Degradation ceremonies in which the status is being socially conferred follow, marking the entry into a specific career path as a deviant. With this confirmation, the person is deemed as either bad, and/or mad, and as incapable of making socially valued decisions. This leads in turn to being stripped of rights, chiefly the right to make decisions concerning oneself. The power to do so is transferred to others (e.g. the justice system, the professionals). Next comes the prescribed social sanction – or treatment – which the person must accept. The aims of the treatment are to prevent further deviancy, to ensure retribution, or to cure an illness which is perceived as the cause of the deviancy, to protect society, and to act as a deterrent for those who may be contemplating a similarly deviant act. Stigma usually follows the initial process of labelling.

A significant minority of people thus labelled is further segregated in an institution. Life led within a segregated community of other deviants and their keepers acts primarily to instil in the residents the self-image of a deviant to the point that it is internalised. Furthermore, the whole process leads to the creation of a one dimensional person, where nothing but the deviancy exists. Thus the deviancy becomes not merely the master status but the only status left. People stop being mothers/fathers, wives/husbands, sons/daughters, friends, workers, citizens, charming or nasty; they are 'prisoners' or 'patients'. The institutional regime is structured in such a way as to prevent friendship and solidarity — often people who lived on the same ward for years do not know each other's names and do not confide in each other. This is achieved without retorting to coercion, but through the repeated message that every resident in the unit is a devalued person. Stopping to think for oneself, stopping to have a private life, stopping to choose what one would eat, drink, put on, read, watch on the television — all of that contributes to the sense of being devalued, and of devaluing oneself. The segregation also marks the rejection by society and often by one's nearest and dearest. In the case of psychiatric hospitalisation initiated by family members the sense of betrayal prevails as well.

It is with this set of beliefs about oneself and the world that people eventually leave the institution. This has led the labelling theorists to propose that the process is largely irreversible, because by the time the person has come out she/he has internalised the devalued image and would continue to present herself/himself to the rest of the world as such, re-enacting a vicious circle.

In addition, this approach offers an understanding of the function of deviancy and its labelling for the non-deviants, i.e. the majority of the population. For them the deviancy of others provides a symbolic and emotional outlet of the same type experienced when observing an acrobat: appreciation of a daring and scaring act, without the need to go through it themselves. For ordinary people labelling acts not only as a deterrent but as a vindication of their own socially valued position, and of the price paid for it in terms of leading a conforming and at times uninteresting life.

The normalisation approach accepts most of this analysis and applies it to people with a disability, as the description of the implications of being devalued presented above indicates (section 1.2). In so doing, it extends the impact of labelling to people who have not been physically segregated, on similar lines to those clarified in the analysis of ageism, racism and gender discrimination.[34]

Yet the SRV approach differs from the labelling approach in two respects. First, it accepts that disabilities are deviations from the norm and that the person is impeded by the disability, and not only by negative social attitudes. Secondly, and more importantly, its protagonists confidently believe that it is possible to *reverse* the impact of the process of labelling and of being devalued, so that the person can become positively valued again. Most of the conceptual work and the practice of normalisation are focused on the reversal of this process. This is made conceptually possible because of the approach's lack of recognition of inherent social control objectives in every society, while such a recognition is implicit in the deviancy school.

The following sections on knowledge are all related to the reversal process and to the objectives of preventing it from happening in the first place, as well as from being repeated, both at the individual and at the societal level. The normalisation approach differs in one more central issue from the focus of symbolic interaction. The provision of adequate material conditions is firmly seen as a precondition to being and feeling valued, and consequently also to the process of reversing the career path of the person with a disability. While it is recognised that the material base is also a reflection of social esteem, within the approach it has an independent status. Only rarely do social interactionism theorists discuss the material base, and then it is usually as a reflection of the symbolic level. This difference is reflected at the knowledge level too, especially in the focus on the structure of physical facilities within the normalisation approach.

### 3.2 Knowledge of the conditions for, and processes of, personal change

Part of the reversal process has to happen at the level of personal change, in which the person who experienced devaluation and internalised it as her true self is able to experience the opposite, i.e. being valued by others and by herself.

Most of the knowledge on personal change comes from psychology, from theories of learning, of personality and motivation, counselling, psychotherapy, and social psychology. Yet because 'people are the product of social relations, with a specific social formation and history'[35] sociological knowledge is indispensable too. This is doubly so because SRV is aimed at introducing change both at the individual and the social levels. The core of personal change is contained in changing the self-identity, if we accept that this identity is the sum-total of our memories of ourselves. The sense of the 'real' self includes the dimensions of uniqueness and distinctiveness; continuity across time and situation; personal worth and social value. When these are violated, as they are in the labelling process, our identity is threatened. Most of the threats come from the outside (e.g. negative social response, being made redundant, being put into an institution), but the person plays a major role in interpreting the clues and in embarking on a specific coping strategy. The threat is experienced at the cognitive, the emotional, and the physical levels. Likewise, the coping response should span more than one level. The coping strategies exist at the intrapsychic level (e.g. a variety of deflection, accommodation and re-evaluation strategies); at the interpersonal level (isolation, negativism, passing, compliance, and opting out); and at the group and intergroup level (e.g. group support, group action, membership of multiple groups).[36] There is no inherent positive or negative value attached to any of these strategies, but they differ in the price which the person may have to pay for employing them, and the degree of personal investment. The choice depends also on the type of threat, the social context, identity structure and cognitive resources.

While the existing literature has focused on the combination of strategies which lead to learned helplessness, relatively little attention has been paid to *invulnerability* factors.[37] Such knowledge would enable the identification and the development of the ability to master one's world better through the use of, for example, selective inconsistency, selective negativism, selective passing, selective compliance and selective alliances.[38]

In facing change, people are facing inconsistency and the unknown. Inevitably, this is perceived as a threat. The crucial issue is whether the change demanded of the person within the SRV approach can also become a challenge, to which positive rewards and an achievable scale of objectives are attached. Thus people need to believe that in the end the change would reduce inconsistency while it would increase self-enhancement.

Social change also influences self-identity, depending on its relevance to the person, the immediacy of involvement in it, and the degree of revision of identity content which the change demands. Applying these concepts to normalisation and people with disabilities, the socially sanctioned normalisation process can be perceived as a process of social change of great personal relevance, characterised by a high degree of immediacy for people who depend on services provided by the community. As such, this process calls for a considerable revision of the identity content of people who have led a segregated or isolated life.

Personal change also has a temporal dimension. Normatively, we expect people to change throughout the life-cycle, and for their identity to incorporate this change. Furthermore, we anticipate that the periods of transition will be threatening, and classify them as 'transitional crisis'.[39] Yet we still have to credit people with disability with the right to be in such a crisis when they enter a new home, when they enter a total institution, and in particular when they leave one. Elsewhere[40] I have suggested that this inevitable threat to personal consistency and continuity should be normalised as much as possible. For being in a transitional crisis implies being in a state of uncertainty, yet entitled to being supported throughout it. The concept of transitional crisis relates also to that of passages and rites of passage, including status passage (e.g. from being single to being married, divorced, employed, unemployed, deviant, ordinary person), all of which are waiting to be used by the normalisation approach for the purpose of personal change.

### 3.3  The detailed knowledge concerning the acquisition of skills for ordinary living

This knowledge comes primarily from education, psychology and physiotherapy, though often knowledge from other sources is useful (e.g. the use of computers for people who cannot write in the usual way). It is based on the commonsensical knowledge of how we all acquire skills in childhood and later in life, focusing on enhancing the motivation to do so and on devising a gradual pace with inbuilt achievable subgoals. In considering motivation, attention is paid to potential obstacles at the level of self-perception and in terms of specific skills. You cannot open a bank account if you cannot sign your name properly, if you have never been to a bank, if you do not have money which you control, if you walk into the bank shabbily dressed; and there is no point in opening an account if you don't know how basic banking works. Opening a bank account is a significant step in terms of individual empowerment in a modern world. It can be a realistic incentive for some people and includes the need for social interaction. In an interesting example, Henry[41] tells the story of how a large group of ex-patients, currently living on the premises of an old psychiatric hospital~in Turin in a loose communal substructure, have been introduced to modern banking by the local bank branch clerks. A process of discussing the pros and cons of a joint account, of electing representatives with signing powers, of deciding on a spending hierarchy, unfolded. The clerks were amazed at the ease with which people who lived all their adult life in a segregating institution took to using their local bank services.

With the exception of aversion 'therapy', behaviour modification and social skills training have a lot to offer in developing positive ordinary living skills and in getting rid of habits which are neither normative nor culturally valued.[42] All good skills training schemes incorporate the different levels of our existence, namely, the cognitive, the emotional, the physical and the social. The normalisation literature has an impressive range of good examples of such a training which follows closely the value base of the approach.

Learning how to live in a group situation is usually part of our everyday socialisation, but given the devalued experiences which many people with disabilities had in group situations, it is necessary to focus on this aspect as a differentiated part of skills for ordinary living. The knowledge base for it comes from commonsensical understanding, as well as from social psychology and sociology.[43]

### 3.4   *Understanding processes of attitudinal change*

The call for attitudinal change as an integral part of normalisation has been one of the hallmarks of the approach. If it is to happen then knowledge of the processes involved are a necessary.

The discussion above concerning personal change is highly relevant here too, because attitudinal change parallels change in self-identity, as are the interrelationships between social change and self-perception.

Attitudes function as ideologies, namely, as guidelines to action and as symbolic acts. These are elements of crucial importance in the context of reversing the process of social devaluation, even though they do not come instead of material conditions and concrete action. Attitudes include cognitive, affective and behavioural components which are interrelated in everyday life, but each of which would need to be reinforced separately and collectively in a change process.[44] Successful attempts at changing prejudice have demonstrated that consciousness raising is necessary as a first step. While it may be highly effective as a tool of change for people who suffer from prejudice, it is insufficient to effect a real change in those who either believe in it or are undecided. These two groups need to be presented with a more involved incentive in order to start to question their beliefs. This could be a media campaign, a close personal encounter, or an encounter relayed to them by a source they trust personally. Thus volunteers working with people with disabilities are a much more influential source of attitudinal change among their circle of family and friends than a television programme or a lecture by a professional.

In the case of people with disabilities, it is important to remember what it is about them which lay people experience as threatening, in order to target the attitudinal change.

This is where the labelling approach is useful, and where essays such as Susan Sontag's *Illness as a Metaphor*, and autobiographical novels such as Christopher Nolan's *Under the Eye of the Clock* and Christy Brown's *My Left Foot* are both powerful and informative.[45] They illustrate how the illness and disability of others remind those lucky enough not to suffer from them of their own fragility, of the apprehension that they, too, will be inflicted, of the gut fear of being at close quarters with suffering, reminding people of their own suffering experiences which they have hoped to bury for good. Yet each of us has experiences of empathy and each of us is capable of transcending our fears and suffering into empathy, provided we feel safe enough in doing so. The safety net required seems to be related to the provision of personal examples by professionals and important figures, and to fostering solidarity with people who are disabled, rather than benevolence and charity.

There are several groups which should be targeted for attitudinal change, such as politicians, the media and informal carers. However, because of limited space, only the attitudinal change of professionals will be looked at.

*Professionals* constitute perhaps the single most important group in terms of the power to determine the lives of people with disabilities and the future of the normalisation approach, which stands to lose some of its power in the process.

Atkinson has illustrated not only the importance of service providers for users, but also the changes in roles which take place in the move from a hospital to a community-based service.[46]

SRV presents a challenge to traditional professional views as it discredits cherished beliefs about disability, deviancy, people with disabilities, professional expertise, professional power, professional conduct, segregation and integration.

In particular the approach challenges the perception of people with disabilities as inferior to those without them, as passive recipients of charity and professional wisdom, as having nothing to give but only to take, as needing care but unable to care for themselves or for others. In so doing, the accepted divide between professionals and users, between the givers and those in need is threatened.

Professionals come to their basic training course with their own life experiences and values. Many people enter the caring professions because they feel an affinity with people who suffer and because they would like to give to others. In the process of training, however, they are usually discouraged from expressing this affinity and from exploring its base. Instead, they are expected to channel it into the professional mould of relationships with clients and ways of thinking about them. To date, this mould is dominated by the perception of people with disabilities as weaklings. While weaknesses, vulner-abilities, disability and disadvantage are focused upon, the strength, the invulnerabilities, abilities and the advantages are being systematically discarded. As a social work educator, I am well aware that the motivation for this emphasis is to bring trainees to be attentive to the client's needs and to internalise professional knowledge for it to become part of their intuitive response. However, basic human empathy may be lost in this process. Moreover, the client is usually not encouraged to state what she sees as her/his needs; these are translated into the professional perspective, which may or may not coincide with that of the client. Current research exemplifies how wide the gap is between these two perspectives for any type of client.[47] The main issues emerging concern how to change professionals' views into accepting the client as a valid partner in the help process, and the user's right and ability to an ordinary life.

Professional training is known to be a powerful resocialisation process because the trainee is exposed to a massive dose of new knowledge and experience, provided by those whose judgement s/he wants to emulate. Thus the main source of primary change in professional attitudes is at the training level, where the trainers' attitudes require to be changed first. Most professions operate from a paradigm of knowledge which has been legitimised sometime ago by eminent members of that profession and by society. Such paradigms change when there is a legitimation crisis and when an alternative to the accepted paradigm is proposed by alternative sources of legitimation. A egitimation crisis[48] can begin when professional burnout is used to examine whether the current professional answers are satisfactory, and when some important answers are found to be wanting. For example, this process has already led to the relatively widespread recognition in professional circles of the damage done by institutionalisation.

Usually, the response to being in such a crisis is similar to that described as a coping strategy when one's identity is threatened, namely, to deflect the threat, to close ranks, and to decry that those who are doubting the validity of the paradigm are ignorant, charlatans, and uncaring.

Thus Basaglia describes what has happened in Gorizia (the first town in which the Italian psychiatric reform began):

> The technicians, who normally represented those values, began to reject their role as functionaries of consent, refusing to endorse and legitimise class discrimination and the transformation of their work and assistance into violence. In creating the conditions for a patient's needs to resurface and be met, a crisis was produced for those who entrusted the technicians with an opposite mission . . . by refusing to be the keepers of these suppressed individuals, by trying to stimulate those vital subjective capacities that had been destroyed or forgotten, the technicians had already chosen to side with those they were delegated to oppress, even with the uncertainty that this choice involved.[49]

A legitimation crisis creates uncertainty which can be borne out if the professionals come to know a better alternative, one which is in line with their original values and which offers improved answers. They are ready to listen to alternatives if these are presented by people they trust, preferably professionals whose integrity is not in doubt, who speak the same language as they do and who have been trained similarly, but who have broken out of the mould. How do individual professionals break out of this powerful mould? Often they are outsiders in at least one important sense; this may be the knowledge of other cultures, coming from a different disciplinary background, and remaining an intellectual as well as a technician-professional.

Apart from the change in the paradigm, professionals change their attitudes in the same way as lay people do, because they, too, are first and foremost people.

## 3.5    Organisational change

Organisational change is necessary for the creation of the non-institutionalised support structures in which the SRV approach can be implemented. Its objective is to ensure the integration, participation and empowerment of people with disabilities in ordinary life. Participation and empowerment, however, are often absent from ordinary settings, hence a more general social change is required.

### Knowledge for organisational change

The knowledge base underlying the understanding of processes and methods of organisational change comes primarily from the theory and practice of organisations and their management within not-for-profit and for-profit settings.

Some elements from the experience of for-profit organisations are valuable for the welfare services which are the focus of the normalisation approach. These include operational autonomy to encourage entrepreneurship, simple form staff, and continued contact with customers, hailed as some of the most important attributes of outstanding performers in the American business world.[50]

Yet the value of this knowledge is limited because in for-profit organisations people are no more than a dispensable tool, whereas in the SRV approach they are both the main tool and the objective of the organisation.

All organisations face change at some stage and good ones are prepared for it. Most welfare organisations have in-built mechanisms which prevent structural change from being a natural response. These include their social control function, bureaucratic inertia, fear of change and of losing power, and a workforce lacking in training to expect change as part of the ordinary challenge of the work.

The most useful knowledge base comes from analysing good examples of technological and social change, including those of public participation (discussed in Chapter 6) and deinstitutionalisation.[51]

The importance of staff participation in consultation and decision-making was brought home to me in researching how three teams of social workers were facing the closure of the London psychiatric hospital in which they worked. The teams were similar in size, in being employed by local authorities social services departments in boroughs of very similar political affinity, in training and in age distribution. Furthermore, the teams operated in the same hospital where they all felt marginalised by professionals from other disciplines. At the end of the study, some eighteen months later, only one team was growing in numbers and responsibilities. The other two were reduced by two-thirds, unable to provide the minimum service and low in morale. The main factor to emerge was that the teams differed at the level of their organisational structure. The more successful team worked in a department where administrative and decision-making responsibilities were delegated and greater autonomy was allowed, even encouraged. After an unsuccessful start in which closure work was allocated to only two workers, it was agreed that all team members would be involved in it. By so doing, a fuller participation in the challenge faced by the closure was achieved. Disempowered professionals cannot be effective in empowering their clients, or in representing their agency to other agencies. Although lofty sounding, a *'culture of change'* is essential to encourage service providers to have a positive attitude towards the possibility of change. This is doubly true in the case of ideas initiated by users or informal carers. It relates primarily to the creation of a climate in the organisation or community in which change is a welcomed term. Yet experience shows that this in itself is insufficient to ensure either the direction of change or its method.

Innovation calls for a clear vision, a detailed hierarchy of objectives and the means of achieving them. It requires a barrier analysis of the political map and a strategy of how to handle the political angle.[52] Leadership, modelling by personal example, backing those who are trying to innovate, motivating a whole team rather than parts of it, creating expected and especially unexpected alliances, hyped motivation and a sense of challenge are the main necessary ingredients. These have to be coupled with risk analysis, developing means of taking responsibility for the risks, and ensuring that the necessary resources for the change are secured.[53] Because the first bout of enthusiasm can so easily evaporate after the first few obstacles, it is of crucial importance to built-in successes, in the form of achievable subobjectives, into the process of innovation. The ability to change tactics in order to overcome hostile agents who, after the initial stage, are likely to use the same rhetoric with a very different aim and meaning attached to it is also important.

Holding all these features together is not an easy task. Support structures beyond achievable success for the innovators need to be part of the in-built system, together with a structure of continuous incentives for all of those involved in the endeavour. Pitching the vision at the right level for the targeted group is not merely a public relations stunt. Only people who share the same broad cultural affinity with their audience are likely to find the right level, even if what they are demanding is far beyond the present limitations of that audience. What they are touching upon (often intuitively, but at times gambling consciously) are the relevant strands in a changing social context. Thus Pinel in eighteen-century France was appealing to the readiness to liberate a number of other categories of people when he freed psychiatric patients from their chains. In order to change the structure of the psychiatric system, Psichiatria Democratica in Italy, during the 1960s and the 1970s, was openly creating alliances with students, women and workers, all of whom were attempting to become more empowered than they were before. Bank-Mikkelson in Denmark (in the 1950s) and Wolfensberger in North America (in the 1960s and 1970s) were utilising the readiness to extend citizens' rights to people with learning difficulties which was related to equal rights for women and ethnic minorities.

Do we therefore need to wait for the right social context to be there first? If, as I do, you believe in feedback, then starting with normalisation-oriented organisational change initiative may be the right trigger for a feedback chain of social change; you never know!

## References

1.  Nirje, B., 'The Normalisation Principle and Its Human Management Implications', in Kugel, R. and Wolfensberger, W. (eds), *Changing Patterns in Residential Services for the Mentally Retarded*, (Washington: President's Committee on Mental Retardation, 1969) pp. 255–87.
2.  Wolfensberger, W., 'Social Role Valorisation: A Proposed New Term for the Principle of Normalisation', *Mental Retardation*, vol. 21, no. 6, 1983, pp. 234–9.
3.  Ryan, J. and Thomas, F., *The Politics of Mental Handicap*, (London: Free Association Books, 1987) p. 149.
4.  Rothman, D., *The Discovery of the Asylum: Social Order and Disorder in the New Republic* (Boston: Little, Brown, 1971).
5.  Wing, J.K., 'Institutionalism in Mental Hospitals', *British Journal of Social and Clinical Psychology*, vol. 1, pp. 38–51.
6.  Barton, R., *Institutional Neurosis* (Bristol: Wright, 1959).
7.  Goffman, I., *Asylum* (New York: Doubleday, 1961).
8.  Foucault, M., *Madness and Civilization* (London: Tavistock, 1972); Basaglia, F., *L'istituzione Negata* (Rome: Einaudi, 1968).

9. Scheper-Huges, N. and Lovell, A.M. (eds), *Psychiatry Inside Out: Selected Writings of Franco Basaglia* (New York: Columbia University Press, 1988).

10. Olshansky, S., 'Changing Vocational Behaviour Through Normalisation', in Wolfensberger, W. (ed.), *The Principle of Normalisation in Human Services* (Toronto: National Institute of Mental Retardation, 1972).

11. Basaglia, F., *L'istituzione Negata*, see 8 above. Rotelli, F. 'Changing Psychiatric Services in Italy', in Ramon, S. (ed.), *Psychiatry in Transition* (London: Pluto Press, 1988) pp. 182–90; Del Giudice, G., Evaristo, P. and Reali, M., 'How Can Mental Hospitals Be Phased Out?' in S. Ramon, ibid., pp. 199–207.

12. Williams, P. and Tyne, A., 'Exploring Values as the Basis for Service Development', in Towell, D. (ed.) *An Ordinary Life in Practice* (London: King's Fund Publications, 1987) pp. 23–31.

13. Wolfensberger, W., 'The Definition of the Principle of Normalisation', see 10 above.

14. Gramsci, A., *Selections from the Prison Notebooks* (New York: International Publishers, 1971); Castel, R., Castle, F. and Lovell, A.M., *The Psychiatric Society* (New York: Columbia University Press, 1982).

15. Bank-Mikkleson, N.E., 'A Metropolitan Area in Denmark: Copenhagen', in Kugel, R. and Wolfensberger, W. (eds), *Changing Patterns in Residential Services for the Mentally Retarded*, see 10 above, pp. 227–54.

16. Salvi, E. and Cecchini, M., 'Children with Handicaps in Ordinary Schools', in Ramon, S. (ed.), *Psychiatry in Transition*, see 11 above, pp. 138–46.

17. Wolfensberger, W., 'Normalising Activation for the Profoundly Retarded and/or Multiply Handicapped', see 10 above, p. 127.

18. Oliver, M. *The Politics of Disablement* (London: Macmillan, 1969). For an interesting discussion of these issues see: Stainton, T., 'The Conceptualisation of Disability: The Dilemma of Difference', paper presented at the London School of Economics Philosophy, Politics and Literature Seminar, 6 March 1990.

19. Perske, R., 'The Risk of Dignity', see 10 above, pp. 194–206.

20. Laing, R.D., *Self and Others* (London: Tavistock, 1971).

21. Timms, N., *Values in Social Work: An Inquiry* (London: Routledge & Kegan Paul, 1984).

22. Wolfensberger, W., 'The Definition of the Principle of Normalisation', see 10 above, pp. 6–9.

23. Race, D., 'Normalisation: Theory and Practice', in Malin: N. (ed.) *Community Care Reassessed* (London: Croom Helm, 1987) pp. 62–79.

24. O'Brien, J., *Against Pain as a Tool in Professional Work on People with Severe Disability* (London: Kings's Fund Centre, 1988).

25. *People First of Washington*. Officer Handbook. (Salem, Oregon: People First International, 1984).

26.  Hinchbold, D. and Harris, N. (ed.), *The Patients' Case: Views from Experience: Living Inside and Out of a Psychiatric Hospital* (Rossendale: Community Psychiatric Nurses Association, 1988). See also 11 above.

27.  Soyer, P., 'The Right to Fail', in McDermott, R. (ed.), *Self Determination* (London: Routledge & Kegan Paul, 1975).

28.  Perske, R., 'The Dignity of Risk', see 10 above, pp. 194–206.

29.  Tranchina, P. and Basaglia, F. (eds), *Autobiografia di un Movimento 1961–1979* (Unione Province Italiane, Regione Toscana, Ammistrazione Provinciale di Arezzo, 1979).

30.  Freire, P., *The Pedagogy of the Oppressed* (London: Lawrence & Wishart, 1972).

31.  O'Brien, J., *Framework for Accomplishment* (Decatur, Georgia: Responsive Systems Associates, 1988).

32.  For a recent study see: Howe, D., *The Consumers' View of Family Therapy* (Aldershot: Gower, 1989).

33.  See 7 above, and Mead, G.H., *Mind, Self and Society* (Chicago: University of Chicago Press, 1934); Becker, H. (ed.), *Outsiders* (Glencoe: The Free Press, 1962); Scheff, T., *Labelling Mental Illness* (Englewood Cliffs, NJ: Prentice-Hall, 1975); Goffman, I., *Stigma* (Harmondsworth: Penguin, 1963).

34.  Pateman, C., *The Disorder of Women* (Oxford: Policy Press, 1989); Ungerson, C., *Policy is Personal* (London: Tavistock, 1987).

35.  Leonard, P., *Ideology and Personality: Towards a Materialist Understanding of the Individual* (London: Macmillan, 1984).

36.  Breakwell, G.M., *Coping with Threatened Identities* (London: Methuen, 1986); Breakwell, G.M., (ed.) *Threatened Identities* (Chichester: Wiley, 1983); Pearlin, L.I. and Schooler, C., 'The Structure of Coping', *Journal of Health and Social Behaviour*, vol. 19, 1978, pp. 2–21.

37.  Rosehan, D.L. and Seligman, M.E.P., *Abnormal Psychology* (New York: Norton, 1984). See also Leonard's concept of resistance in 35 above.

38.  Garmezy, N. and Rutter, M. (ed.), *Stress, Coping and Development in Children* (New York: McGraw-Hill, 1983).

39.  Golan, N., *Being in Transition* (New York: Columbia University Press, 1982).

40.  Ramon, S., 'The Relevance of Symbolic Interaction Perspectives to the Conceptual and Practice Construction of Leaving a Psychiatric Hospital', *Social Work and Social Science Review*, forthcoming.

41.  Henry, P., 'Towards a Rehabilitative Psychiatry, see 11 above, pp. 82–9.

42.  Hudson, B. and MacDonald, E., *Behavioural Social Work* (London: Macmillan, 1986); Trower, P. (ed.), *Handbook of Social Skills Training* (Oxford: Pergamon Press, 1986).

43.  Mugny, G., *The Power of Minorities* (London: Academic Press, 1982); Austin, W.G. and Worchel, S. (eds), *The Social Psychology of Intergroup Relations* (Monterey, Cal.: Brooks/Cole, 1979).

44.  Rokeach, M., *Beliefs, Attitudes and Values* (San Francisco: Jossey-Bass, 1978).

45. Sontag, S., *Illness as a Metaphor* (New York: Random House, 1979); Nolan, C., *Under the Eye of The Clock* (London: Weidenfeld & Nicolson, 1987); Brown, C., *My Left Foot* (London: Mandarin, 1987).

46. Atkinson, D., *Someone to Turn To* (British Institute of Mental Handicap, 1989).

47. Scott, R.A., *The Making of Blind Men: A Study of Socialization* (New York: Sage Foundation, 1969); McCord, W.T., 'From Theory to Reality: Obstacles to the Implementation of the Normalisation Principle in Human Services', *Mental Retardation*, vol. 20, no. 6, 1982, pp. 247–53.

48. Habermas, J., *Legitimation Crisis* (London: Heinemann, 1973); Gleick, J., *Chaos: Making of a New Science* (London: Heinemann, 1989).

49. Basaglia, F., 'Peacetime Crimes: Technicians of Practical Knowledge', see 9 above, p. 146.

50. Peters, T.J. and Waterman, R.H., *In Search of Excellence: Lessons from America's Best-run Companies* (New York: Harper & Row, 1984).

51. Fagence, M.T., *Citizen Participation in Planning* (Oxford: Pergamon Press, 1977); Rossi, P. and Dentler, R., *The Politics of Urban Renewal* (New York: Free Press, 1961); McEwen, J. (ed.), *Participation in Health* (London: Croom Helm, 1983).

52. See 11 above.

53. Stark, J.A., McGee, J.J. and Menolascino, F.J., *International Handbook of Community Services for the Mentally Retarded* (Hillsdale, NJ: Lawrence Erlbaum, 1984) pp. 107–30; Mansell, J., 'Training for Service Development', see 12 above, pp. 129–40. See also 31 above, section on management skills in chapter 3.

'Mutual vulnerability increases as physical and social distance decrease, as weaker people gain control over resources, and as purposes and projects are shared. It grows from a decision to allow the other to become important to us, to touch us personally.'

J. O'Brien, *Against Pain as a Tool in Professional Work on People with Severe Disabilities*

# 2
# The Implications of Normalisation Work for Professional Skills

*David Brandon*

Just what are the professional skills in areas like nursing, social work and psychology, when they seem an amplification of the ordinary social skills possessed (allegedly) by shopkeepers, secretaries and British Rail guards? Can you have paid skills in loving and caring particularly when agencies which employ those same people often manifest contrasting values? How is it possible to encourage professionals to be open and involved when their agencies are frequently closed and oppressive?

McCord puts it starkly.

> In general, agencies operate within a social, political, and economic framework that rewards practices which increase the dependency of deviant people on the human service sector... Human services enact their role as agents of control by addressing themselves to four overriding tasks: (a) pinpointing the deviant characteristics of people through labelling procedures, and thus assuring society that containment is warranted; (b) keeping deviant people isolated so that society experiences neither the embarrassment nor the burden of caring for such persons; (c) keeping deviant people under control so that society can continue to socialize new members to the accepted boundaries of traditional values and norms; (d) perpetuating deviance by teaching people to conform to their deviant status and to willingly accept their own containment.[1]

As a social work teacher, I found that the emphasis in both education and training was rather more on socialisation into organisationally desirable qualities of reliability, respectability and responsibility than on the development of direct skills. Students were training to be soft policemen. They were pulled in many different directions – one way by the needs of distressed customers and another considerably stronger pull, the controlling demands of the bureaucracy which pays them.

Student professionals were taught to keep within the confining social norms of the service. They were taught not to share information, because secrecy held power.

35

'What is it that patients complain of more than anything else in relation to the hospital – "No one told me anything" – "Nobody asked me" – "I don't know." How often one comes across people who have been discharged from hospital, bewildered, still anxious and afraid; disillusioned because the medical magic has not apparently or not yet yielded results, ignorant of what the investigations have shown, what the doctors think, what the treatment has been or is to be, and what the outlook is in terms of life and health.[2]

Skills have more to do with the sheer survival in the health and social services jungle than with the more obvious roles of social workers and nurses. Keeping your head below the bureaucratic parapet and fending off administrators is usually the most valued skill of all. Without those skills, the young professional is easily overwhelmed.

Relationships with colleagues need the skills of liaison and coordination. These relationships were often much more fraught and difficult than those with clients/patients. Professions can be (usually privately) enormously critical of each other. Professor Sidney Brandon looked at Leicestershire community psychiatric nurses' attitudes to their work and colleagues.[3] The twenty-three nurses interviewed were extremely sceptical about other members of the psychiatric team, particularly of consultant psychiatrists, considered 'virtually useless'. They saw social workers as totally redundant and were only slightly more sympathetic to GPs.

The nurses saw their main role in psychotherapy – especially with those patients who had obsessional, compulsive disorders. They did not feel their job should include monitoring patients' medication and compliance. Wolfensberger's sardonic comment that professionals 'generally see their own needs better than they see the needs of the people coming to them for help' is particularly relevant.[4]

In my experience of mental illness services, it was much easier to get professional staff to see 'worried well' young people than old ladies with Alzheimer's syndrome. Whatever 'real nursing' or 'real social work' means, it often coincides with moving away from close contact with very disabled and distressed people, involving what my old friend Kay Carmichael calls 'the flight from pain'. When we attain some control over our work, there is a tendency to retreat from experiences which make us feel impotent, in favour of those which give us the feeling of power and control, however fleeting and illusory that may be.

Existing training methods encourage us to feel most uncomfortable about our vulnerability and fallibility. Our vulnerability is our greatest strength and resource. We can help to heal through a thorough knowledge of personal weakness and damage. Rather than helping to conceal weaknesses, we should be helped on training courses to use those qualities to gain a deeper understanding of what customers are going through. Shamans, the wounded healers, have a long and honourable tradition of healing through their wounds.[5]

The socialisation of professionals inevitably leads to increased social distance. Increasingly, professionals live in different parts of the town or even different towns from their customers. They earn considerably more; live in larger houses in the better areas; drive bigger cars; use polar bear skin filofaxes, making it increasingly difficult to identify with how their customers, who are mainly poor, live.

The initial messages people get when they start 'on the job', particularly from immediate bosses and peer group, are crucial. Frank Thomas writes of his first daunting day as a nursing auxiliary in the 1970s in a large North-West of England mental handicap hospital — early morning exchanges on a ward of over fifty patients.

Nurse: 'Hello shitface, here's your sodding breakfast.'

Charge nurse: 'Tables! Come on, you lot! Get yourselves to your seats! Stand by your seats! Keep quiet. Quiet now! Right, sit down! Green, shut up! What's up with you lot this morning? Any more noise and you'll go to bed at four o'clock. Right, keep the noise down. First table! Come on, get your porridge before it gets cold. Come on, you lazy buggers, we haven't got all day.'

All this at an ear-splitting level.[6]

Early writings on the principle of normalisation were vague about a new vision of professionalism. Some of Wolfensberger's writings on 'social role valorisation' strike a note of deprofessionalisation rather than one of reprofessionalism. However, the implications of the principle help to analyse and comprehend how quickly paid staff learn controlling skills, which often serve as a defence against institutional traumas. Normalisation provides a framework for the conscious adoption of a new set of values, to provide more coherency between what we say and what we do. There is always considerable difference between what we learn and what we are taught as the example above reminds us. At best, training can be a vision of good practice. From day to day experiences of working in a hostel or day centre, frequently, we receive more debased messages.

Professionals are trained to exercise skills within fantasy frameworks of supposedly complex and sophisticated relationships with clients/patients. This can lead to enormous frustrations in which professionals become the victims of huge organisational inconsistencies and hypocrisies. Isabel Menzies Lyth is a psychoanalyst studying the sources of nurses stress. She writes about coping with relationships with patients, the trauma of breaking those relationships and receiving the projection of the patients' anxieties, disgust and depression. It was usually easier to deny the feelings, which hospitals still encourage.

She notes that hospitals traditionally dealt with these problems by moving nurses about. Nurses did not have much responsibility. Despite thorough training and implied expectations of status and autonomy, they performed lists of tasks almost ritualistically. Precise instructions were given and decisions discouraged. Nurses were allowed little discretion. In this way they were relieved of almost all responsibility. Actions were checked and rechecked; decisions were referred upwards, 'leaving staff and students with a very low level of tasks in relation to their ability'. This did little for their self-esteem, personal growth or job satisfaction. They were denied what they wanted and expected from nursing, responsibility and close, caring relationships.[7]

In this unpromising and depressing stale porridge of systems, what are the current notions of professional skills and their underlying assumptions? Rita and Noel Timms suggest that social workers should accomplish five different activities: to conduct interviews with individuals or groups who often face and experience loss and change; to plan and to help others to plan on a basis of the understanding of situations; to offer and to support the delivery of a range of personal services including non-directive and directive counselling to individuals and groups and advocacy; to know, use and criticise the policy of the agency; to record.[8] It sounds a bit like an off-peak radiator system with all power and wisdom going one way.

Anderson suggests that social work is about the resolution of conflict with social norms.[9] The skills should

> put people in touch with existing services; negotiate for people or teach social skills; be open-minded themselves and have a personal enough relationship with people to understand the meaning of unconventional behaviour, and to convey that understanding to others; arrange for services to be extended or for new services to be provided to cover multiple need; attempt to find solutions or encourage others to find

solutions to unsolved problems; publicise and campaign for the adoption of new solutions which have been found.

All that seems paternalistic.

The community nurse will offer special skills as a trainer/teacher of mentally handicapped children and adults, especially in relation to the development of self-help. He will also ensure that parents are helped to participate in the training programmes. Some parents will need advice about general management and physical care, especially if the mentally handicapped member is multiply handicapped. When behaviour problems are present, the CMHN will, in consultation with the team, be able to set up behaviour modification programmes and involve the parents as co-therapists ... The development of special interests by community nurse should also be encouraged.[10]

Here the emphasis is again on the professional as a huge repository of wisdom and the users as imbibers.

Pilgrim is acidic about the contemporary education and skills training of psychologists.

Unfortunately psychology itself has an impersonal tradition which leaves clinical psychologists at the outset of their careers hamstrung by the false hope and security of scientific competence to add to their frequent personal insecurity, which is an intelligible function of relative youth. Technique-oriented workshop manuals peddled by behavioural psychology and psychometric devices are a great comfort to neophyte psychologists but of dubious value to the inevitably complex personal and contextual variation of psychological distress in the real world.[11]

Philip Roos writes about the objectionable characteristics of the medical model which permeates most helping professions.

The relationship between the 'ill' person and the 'healer' is structured so as to foster feelings of helplessness, passivity, and dependency on the part of the former, while generating inappropriate illusions of omnipotence and omniscience on the 'healer's' part. It has been argued that much of the maladaptive behaviour noted in the institutionalised person is a function of the staff's 'therapeutic' interaction.[12]

This is a process towards controlling interference essentially dependent on the infantilisation of consumers. Professionals are trained to play a pale imitation of Icarus — the Greek legend of the mortal man, son of Daedalus, who put on waxen wings and flew too close to the sun until his wings melted and he fell back to the earth. The human costs of the Icarus role are extremely high.

Contrast those modern ideas about professional skills with the simple humanity of Florence Nightingale.

> Apprehension, uncertainty, waiting, expectation, fear of surprise, do a patient more harm than any exertion. Remember he is face to face with his enemy all the time, internally wrestling with him, having long imaginary conversations with him . . . Do not forget that patients are shy of asking. It is commonly supposed that a nurse is there to save physical exertion. She ought to be there to save [the patient] taking thought.[13]

The heart of professionalism is putting oneself in the shoes of the patient — imagining how it is for him or her. I much prefer Nightingale's attempt but difficult to square her dreaming professional aspirations with the harsh realities of Frank Thomas's first day as a ward orderly.

Few definitions of skills start from the users' experience. Users are in a relatively powerless and neglected position. Examine this sensitive passage.

> Traditionally, the hospital patient has been lucky and glad to be looked after, whether an out-patient, casualty, or in-patient. The historical origins of the hospitals are either charity, religious or secular, or the Poor Law authorities. These origins are still detectable in the attitude of hospital staff to their patients: anyone who questions this can verify it for himself unless he is exceptionally fortunate, by simply taking a seat for an hour or two on benches in an out-patient or reception department. The patient and the patient's relatives are face to face not with the doctors but with the panoply of an institution, physical, corporate and social. All the romance, wonder and terror of modern medical science is associated with the hospital and its deep recesses: the hospital has prestige and inspires awe. For good measure, the hospital patient is often for one reason or another helpless.[14]

Enoch Powell wrote that while Minister of Health.

The late Don Bannister, a clinical psychologist, wrote about the seemingly verdant pastures of counselling and psychotherapy. He examined the theme of power.

> Clearly, the relationship between therapist and client is initially neither reciprocal nor equal. If you are the therapist then you and the client sit on either side of your desk, in your office, on your patch. Your presence signifies qualifications, expertise and prestige; the client's presence

signifies that he or she has 'given in', 'confessed failure'. You, as therapist, represent [socially, if not in fact] the healthy ordered life while the client represents 'sickness' and confusion.[15]

These barriers are usually conveniently ignored by professionals. We cherish our hard won fantasies and delusions.

Olshansky cannot ignore these barriers.

First, professionals, by training, are committed to treating pathology and abnormality. One might say they always see pathology and abnormality even where none exists . . . Second, professionals too often develop a sense of superiority to the people they help. Enjoying feelings of superiority, they somehow lose interest and faith in the capacity of their 'inferiors' to change, to grow. Moreover, they expect less from inferior persons . . . Third, professionals tend to see only the 'inner space', the intrapsychic. The only experiences they value are the clinical ones, where they are in control and their contacts are brief. The experiences outside the clinic seem to them of little value . . . Fourth, professionals are imprisoned by habits. They prefer to do what they have done. It is easier and more comfortable to treat pathology as they have been doing and as they have been trained to do. The principle of normalisation is a challenge to change their focus and habits.[16]

How are those habits and traditions to be changed and in what directions and by what means? Normalisation invites us to focus on the nature of change in services rather than on changing the pathology of the devalued individual. We have outlined five major themes – *good relationships; maximising choices; effective participation; personal development and greater mixing.*[17] They provide a complex three-dimensional jigsaw with a few easy shapes covering most of the extensive criteria. They present a challenge for user based services with a coherent philosophical base measured against a clearly outlined outcome. Wolfensberger calls this 'Model Coherency'. There is very little material which tries to sketch out their necessary implications for the training and skills development of professionals.

Presently, we take student professionals right away from their customers for large chunks of their education and training. Their direct experiences are often devalued in training sessions. They are trained in an elitism based on an under current that professionals really know best. Promotion and increased salaries means greater social distance from the customers. Frontline staff are usually the worst paid and the least qualified and experienced.

## Good relationships

We have to provide settings which nourish and support the depth of contact between paid staff and consumers. Professionals are often trained to feel guilty about their relationships with users. Over emotionalism is suspect. Relationships can become emotionally constipated – cool and detached, never offering real friendship, which is considered dangerous and uncool.

Witness this account of fine work in a coronary unit.

> The conflict between professional distance and emotional involvement has been identified as a central problem for nurses in their care of dying patients. While some nurses may attempt to maintain their professional distance, individualised methods of patient care encourage the development of emotional involvement between nurses and their patients. Where such nursing methods are used it is essential that appropriate ways exist of handling problems which such involvement may cause nurses. In the coronary care unit studied, the organisation of nursing work facilitated close and continuing contact between nurses and their patients, thereby increasing the chance that emotional involvement would develop. The death of a patient was not viewed by the nurses as 'failure'; but there were sometimes difficulties for them arising from their involvement with the patient.
>
> One reason which some nurses gave for enjoying work was that it allowed greater involvement with patients than possible in other settings . . . One registered nurse said: 'It's only short-term involvement. It's not like your mum or dad or somebody that you're going to remember the rest of your life. I've probably got emotionally involved with patients whose names I couldn't tell you now. But while they were alive and I was looking after them I was emotionally involved with them. But now it doesn't bother me.'
>
> Despite the costs, emotional involvement by nurses with dying patients was more likely to be positive than negative for both nurse and patient. A system of individualised patient care seems associated with good nursing care of the dying and also, it seems, inevitably creates a certain amount of involvement. It is, however, clear that high levels of involvement may cause difficulties for nurses, and that many nurses therefore endeavour to limit or avoid it.[18]

The implications for training are immense. We need to explore and share our vulnerability – to move away from the macho traditions of our professions. We are not aiming for independent heroes and heroines but for interdependence, with people working in a nourishing environment and trusting more in each others wisdom and skills. That must include more appreciation of users' attainments and more diffusive relationships which allow consumers to make greater contribution to the quality of services. That involves a 180 degree turn in the existing training.

The emphasis needs to be on the skills of openness and flexibility. We need to have access to support and use it. We need to express our difficulties with others and feel confident in sharing. That means working more closely as a team and not being afraid of ignorance and personal limitations. Often ignorance is the only wisdom. There are no real answers to many areas of human suffering except that we eventually and unavoidably fall ill and die. Being strong has to take on a new meaning in the professions. There are none so weak as those who *must* cope with everything.

What kind of support structures will work? Recently, in Holland, I saw some former service users, women who had been depressed, working with professionals in helping others. This helps fuzz the boundaries between helpers and helped. Boundaries become more diffusive. Professionals also felt more able to talk about their distress. Maxwell Jones has written widely about open systems – structures which assist both consumers and staff to be more open and work through changing processes more transparently.[19]

## Maximising choices

Hobson's choice, meaning no real choice at all, is an essential characteristic of many human services. 'You either go into that old people's home or stay in the mess you're already in.' 'No – you can't have another social worker. You're stuck with the one we sent you . . .' Our systems are frequently monopolistic and autocratic. People need to have real and increasing choices as well as meaningful options – increased control over – food, drink, patterns of the day like mealtimes and bedtimes, holidays, sexuality, relationships. All that involves access to resources like money, telephones, transport, friends to share with and help, adequate knowledge and information, social skills and experience, competence with tools, musical instruments, gardening . . . above all, surrounded by people who believe you can do it and what Bob Perske calls the 'dignity of risk'.

People start off by being devalued and labelled 'mentally ill' or 'wheelchair case'. They are shunted off into devalued services which amplify their deviance, herding people with handicaps together in one place with staff who are poorly paid, trained and supported.

Their choices in this increasingly segregated world are narrowed even further. Their poverty, marginalisation, lack of information and increasing feelings of powerlessness extend their feelings of powerlessness.

Choices involve everything from cornflakes to porridge; choosing holidays from Scunthorpe to Tahiti; from stamp collecting to skydiving. They mean actively engaging with the world; being active rather than just reactive; being able to express myself; feeling the impact of me on the universe and vice versa; becoming a person of value with influence and power.

Staff need to communicate *realistic optimism.* We must select innovative people, full of ideas and possibilities. Practical dreamers. They need training in practical visions, constructive options and how to work towards them. The services must give the staff a direct feeling of making choices, of having control over their lives, instead of feeling like a private in the Red Army.

Choices are widened through us having respect for others so that they can learn and expand. Staff also need help in widening peoples experience and possibilities for ordinary living and independence. If they are to model good practice, they need to experience it. Users are usually going to need real work and real wages to have effective choices in our desperately materialistic society.

Our concept of choice is widened further by the Avoider movement amongst people with disabilities.[20] These are pioneering individuals and groups of people who distance themselves from services run by professionals. They want cash not staff. They want their own services to free themselves of the colonialism of able-bodied people (developed further in Chapter 5). It has some parallels with the separatist branch of the Feminist Movement. It doubts fundamentally that professionals can ever engage in a genuine partnership with people who have disabilities.

This has links with service brokerage developed in Canada, particularly in British Columbia and Alberta, which gives devalued people the opportunity to finance their own services. As in the advocacy movement, it produces a new kind of professional — the service broker, who fixes deals for people with disabilities.[21]

Brian Salisbury (Broker):

> As a Broker, I'm an agent for the person whom I act on behalf of. I don't do things to the person. My whole role is designed to on the one hand identify needs and on the other hand take the vision of those needs and translate it into what's appropriate and obtainable in the community. What I really do is walk through the community system . . . The

greatest sense of fulfilment or reward that I get as a Broker is the empowerment of other people.[22]

As I saw in Canada recently, some users are rapidly acquiring the skills of service providers. They are able to hire and sometimes to fire staff.

## Effective participation

We have to see the development of real democracy within human services so that users exercise their rights as citizens even when entering an old people's home or a psychiatric hospital. Too many devalued people go from relative democracy into services which are the political equivalents of Central American republics and lose any rights they formerly held.

An important study by Lindsay Dyer describes the non-citizenship of many devalued people.

> People who live in psychiatric hospitals may vote but only if they meet certain conditions, which others, who live in the community – with or without a mental illness –, do not have to comply with. The Representation of the People Act 1983 requires residents of psychiatric hospitals to complete a special form – a 'Patients' Declaration' – which, in formal language, requires details of name, age, address of the hospital where they live and the address of the place where they would be living if they were not in hospital or any address in the United Kingdom (other than a mental hospital) where they were resident in the past. This is the address for which they will be registered to vote... In 1984, only 319 patients (6.3%) of a total psychiatric hospital population in the North West out of 6,195, were registered to vote, and one whole hospital population (including residential staff!) was disenfranchised. By 1987, the position had worsened: only 247 patients (4.8%) of a total hospital population of 5,210 were on the electoral register and two whole hospital populations were disenfranchised. There is a substantial difference between rhetoric and reality. The Ministers statement (Mrs Edwina Currie) in November 1987 (Hansard 12 November 1987) that the 1983 Act ensures that informal patients in mental hospitals are able to register as electors is, at the very least, unconvincing.[23]

The tide slowly turns as some professionals learn skills of sharing power. Participation by users in the selection of staff is an important element. Cardiff has pioneered some strands. Frost describes their experiences.[24]

Our biggest mistake was to assume that involving people with mental handicaps in selecting staff would cause a great problem. If there have been difficulties, these lie exclusively with those of us who live with the daily illusion, confirmed by our job titles and salaries and a host of other signs and symbols, that we think, as others may think, we know what we are doing . . . Twenty seven staff appointments ranging from co-ordinators of community mental handicap teams to care assistants in community living schemes and community support workers have jointly been made with people with mental handicaps.

Harper writes of the involvement of people with learning difficulties in service planning groups in Clwyd.[25] 'Initially, staff were challenged. It was all new and strange. Staff were having to acquire new skills in self advocacy, reorganising traditional committee structures, new approaches to participating in meetings so that consumers were not dominated and had time to express their points of view.'

Clwyd and Cardiff provide excellent examples of some power sharing. Devalued people are being encouraged and trained to speak out for themselves — self-advocacy. Current professional training offers little guidance and some barriers. Student professionals can be trained to be open to radical innovation. Services need to respect users gifts and wisdom and provide adequate information; machinery for consultation; for the development of both staff and users skills in areas like self-advocacy and assertion; access to independent representation as in citizen advocacy for example.

Professionals are often fearful of power sharing. They came in to social work, nursing or medicine to take up quasi-parental positions. They may not know how to cope with greater equality, more brotherly/sisterly relations. Such relationships may seem threatening and less controllable. They lose influence. Users will probably make decisions that are seemingly foolish and risky when the role of professionals, for so long, has been to control, to protect and to cosset. The structures in which they operate hold them directly accountable for things which go wrong. Given no radical changes in organisational structures, reasonable risks going wrong may lead to the blame of the professionals.

## Personal development

The personal development both users and workers is among the most difficult tasks for our services. We are moving very slowly away from negative 'you can't' philosophies to seeing our customers as achievers. All kinds of packages like individualised programme planning and case management can assist but packages are not enough. What is required is a substantial attitude and skill shift.

When we meet ordinary people they talk about what they and their families do, who they are. We explore each other's natures and activities. If we visit someone's home or office, the rooms usually say a thousand things about the person who lives there – that they are tidy, read books about Arctic exploration, like Mozart rather than the Beatles, have a preference for strong colours rather than pastels, greens rather than reds, comfy furniture. We ask how they spend their days; what kinds of friends; what sports they watch or play, accomplishments, etc. We discover something about their individuality – comparing and contrasting between us and the people we know. 'They are like us.' 'They are different from us.'

What makes us feel worthwhile and valued is a complex jigsaw. Perhaps we have firm convictions about religion and/or politics. 'Being a Christian or a Muslim' gives a sense of identity and common faith with others. We are part of a group of fellow believers, attending services, worship, study groups. Perhaps we gain confidence from skills in woodwork, car maintenance, gardening, running, cooking. Some people find confidence in their knowledge: they know about geography, German, maths, chemistry.

Most find confidence in relationships. We are loved by others; feel warm about close friends; feel nourished; feel attractive. Most of us own cherished possessions – things which have a sentimental value – an engagement ring, a favourite pen given as a present by Mum, photos, records. We feel we have personal attributes. We are kind, generous, patient, funny – at least some of the time. We feel influential. People respect us. We have responsibility. We get paid money for things we do. We are employed. We have a wage packet. We may get promoted within the organisation. We are members of important clubs, building society, American Express card holders. All this helps the building of what and who we feel we are in this world and the ways in which others behave to us. Without that complicated matrix of reference points how does anyone know what to make of us?

Normalisation reminds us that the blossoming of individual selves is difficult in the 'special' services. People usually don't feel 'special'. Both users and staff are used to marginalised groups. Devalued people are looked after often by devalued and poorly paid staff. Talent and initiative are knocked out of them by an extensive and brutal system. So-called helping cultures can be extremely oppressive, rendering most people passive and ritualised. Not only users get infantilised and institutionalised, it happens to staff as well.

In exploring the normalisation principle, we need skills which take us away from the demands of services towards seeing the individuality of Alice and Fred. That means moving towards a view of people as lovers, tenants, house owners, workers rather than as patients, bedwetters, deviants, self-mutilators. These skills help the emergence of individuality and personal development and achievements.

That emergence needs core counselling training for all staff. We need to listen and respect individual wishes and differences in ways which have not so far been evident. *Good listening*, helping people to construct their visions for their own increasingly independent existence, are vital components in professional help. It needs an ability to see far beyond the wheelchair, the crutches and the dark glasses into the person's true nature and potential.

The inherent visions of professionalism contained in Gentle Teaching (working with people with 'behaviour problems') from Nebraska in the USA are impressive. It teaches the value and goodness of human presence and participation leads to bonding rather than bondage. Bonding encourages mutual liberation – a posture of solidarity, becoming at one with the other, closeness, warmth, acceptance and tolerance.

> At the heart of social interactions lies equity. At the start of relationships with people who have severe learning difficulties, giving and receiving are necessarily imbalanced. We will give much and receive little – creating participation when it is not wanted and giving reward when it is not appreciated. Ancient and savage feelings may bubble up from our being. As greater bonding takes place, that inequity lessens if allowed and teaching strategies which move us away from mutual human liberation avoided.
>
> Our central purpose is reward teaching – both as an end and a a means. It completely eliminates the need for persons to hurt themselves or others. Distancing is replaced by interdependence; compliance is replaced by reciprocity and respect; macho independence replaced by interdependence. A pivotal component is redirection. It consists of teaching responses that refocus the interactional flow from undesirable to rewarding interactions.
>
> Gentle teaching approaches involve a constant review of our goals, creative teaching skills and persevering effort. It is crucial to create opportunities to give reward. If that only involves ignoring maladaptive

behaviours, it will not work. Reward giving and eventually reward sharing comprise the core of our actions.[26]

## Genuine mixing

This is about integration with non-paid and non-devalued people. Most existing services encourage segregation and congregation so that disabled people feel weird to 'ordinary' people who have had little contact with them. Ordinary people also experience a segregated education system: segregated away from people with disabilities.

Mixing means access to buildings through necessary ramps and wide doors at times when others, who are not handicapped, are using the facilities, with understanding staff to help if necessary. It means receiving respect, good manners and esteem from others within a society which has a positive image of handicapped people; having the opportunity for a satisfying private life with meaningful relationships; being a citizen with legal status and opportunities for growth, maturing and self-fulfilment; living in a society with structures and forms that assist all kinds of integration, primarily through ordinary and valued services.[27]

Mixing involves narrowing the social distance between staff and consumers. It means changing congregated provision for devalued people into more general use for a wider variety of 'ordinary' and valued people. It means encouraging users to use unsegregated facilities like art galleries, ordinary buses and taxis, snooker halls and moving away from services which only provide for 'special groups' like Gateway clubs, Special Olympics, psychiatric clubs. For staff it will involve major changes, often helping people to make use of their networks – painting clubs, community contacts, even friends and relatives.

Staff must learn skills to help access. They learn to be effective bridges into wider neighbourhood and community facilities. They are less central to the support of the devalued person and more facilitating of other relationships, which are more important over the long term. Instead of being omnipotent providers, like the professional definitions we looked at earlier, they make ordinary contacts with valued facilities from libraries to community centres.

Martin and Parrott saw that many young people with learning difficulties lived very isolated lives in Sheffield. They started a project to use the city's recreation facilities which had far-reaching benefits. They produced pen profiles of all young adult people known to workers in north-west Sheffield. Many wanted to learn to play snooker so eight young men joined a class with an adult education tutor and social worker. With the skills learned, most people joined snooker clubs from this class and played with ordinary people. The development of this system has led to a wide range of people exploring different leisure pursuits – sewing, car maintenance, adult literacy, cookery.

> We have come to recognise the value of local group working in supporting individuals who have needs in common. From initial contact with three young women who had low self confidence and lacked friends, we identified eight young women in the area with similar needs. We responded by running a short life assertion group to discuss common problems, finding new and more constructive ways of emotional expression and supported friendships.[28]

All this material has fundamental consequences for the skills required for the managing of services. In many ways it increases the extent of chaos. Creativity comes from a mess where unexpected and inspirational connections can be made. Managers need to welcome chaos and live comfortably with it rather than attempting a clean-up. Instead of traditionally setting clear guidelines, and developing rather rigid categories and working out prescribed goals, it throws the windows and doors wide open.

Managers under normalised systems are trying to make sense of services which constantly run into storms and gales. They are no longer organisational kings and queens attempting to control people and resources but more like ocean surfers, riding on the tops of huge waves and trying to stay balanced. Services are fluid. They reach into the wider community and ordinary valued facilities. Services try to minimise the user's dependence on them.

Managers are no longer objective outsiders, making important command decisions from deep bunkers, but mediating *facilitators* intrinsically involved in a complex system of stated values and principles which apply to them as well as to others like staff and users. Issues of moral coherence and consistency are important here. They are modelling the necessary qualities of care and openness rather than simply invoking others to do so. Invoking others to attain high moral standards is always much easier than simple practice. Managers don't stand outside anything.

*They need vision* to see beyond the day to day hurly burly. They are making links between broad principles and values and the concrete elements of provision, anticipating practical tensions. They encourage vision, innovation and flexibility in others. Others are allowed and even encouraged to provide leadership. Current management styles tend to paranoia and to stifle innovation.

*Managers try to discern elements of structure* in the chaos and mess rather than imposing ideologies and dogmatism from outside. They need a quality of beginners mind, a don't knowingness, which is flowing and accepting rather than shaping and boxing. Events write on them rather than the other way around. They are mediating between necessary and diffusive structures and the individual needs of users in creative tension. That is a considerable balancing act as there is a constant shortfall between aspirations and existing finite resources. Everyone feels responsible for hard and difficult decisions. Alienation is lessened so that the organisation belongs to all rather than being owned by powerful and distant others. Existing large services are broken up into smaller chunks.

Management is characterised by positive and warm support. Workers feel valued and encouraged by their seniors who have their interests at heart. They are perceived as unique individuals each making special contributions to the service. They identify existing organisational principles – both implicit and explicit. Typically, that is a misty maze full of skeletons. Most organisations are constipated by their own history. Managers face the implications of often oppressive historical circumstances ('We've always done it this way'); and facilitate the identification of all the hidden agendas, power games, relationships which block more user-based strategies. It takes courage to tackle issues which are personally and structurally so full of fear.

A major skill lies in developing structures which encourage *open systems* so that staff and users feel listened to and valued; able to make positive contributions. Their voices are heard so frustrations are minimised. Injustices are tackled by all. Equality becomes a practical and everyday experience rather than some distant and highflown principle.

Managers move away from the polarised authoritarianism *towards genuine power sharing*. They are natural democrats and vehicles for common aspirations. Systems open up so people can see more clearly how important decisions are made. Senior staff are effective groupworkers, exploring avenues of compromise and synthesis.

The organisational structures have a quality of transparency. Organisations become more like open communities where people share their hopes and dreams and more emphasis is placed on cooperation than on competition. The growth in community takes us gradually away from obsessions with self-serving and more towards a concern with the general welfare.

Managers need *considerable communication skills*, particularly in listening rather than simply talking. They are trying to understand ways of using and expanding organisational resources into serving people's deep needs. Process becomes more important than prescribed goals. Much of their role is reactive in nature. They are reacting to the aspirations and dreams of users, relatives and junior staff. They have a gentleness which encourages others to express their pain and sorrow as well as their courage and diligence.

They are constantly trying to *push the arenas for major decision-making downwards*. The further down the decisions are made, the nearer power comes to the user. He or she can influence more substantially the nature and quality of services being offered. In order to prevent the Icarus syndrome, flying too near to the sun, managers must keep close contact with users who articulate the most valued and earthy criticism and are, rightly, constantly moving the goal posts. User experiences are the major ingredient in any evaluation of the service.

There can be no place for the Frank Sinatra approach to social policy – 'I did it my way'. Changes must come from the education and participation of all. One immense danger is that normalisation becomes yet another form of professional evangelism. That means that we come back from PASS courses with the magic Wolfensberger stone tablets and simply tell the various stakeholders how it ought to be. When they argue back, it is seen as resistance.

Normalisation reminds of the dangers of certain forms of evangelism. It must help, guide and educate us all – people with disabilities, their families, various professionals, ordinary folk in the community. If we and they don't have a real say in the newly developed services, we will never feel they belong to us, never feel that they are ours. The centuries of alienation will continue.

The challenges for new kinds of skills in new kinds of settings have to be faced by me as well as by something abstractly called professionals. I make some of my daily living out of working with devalued groups, nowadays as a freelance. I have an experience of being psychiatrised and some years of disabling back problems. (We are all in between periods of relative disability if we live to be old enough.) Both sets of experiences of the relevant psychiatric and orthopaedic services left me feeling that no one listened and that the service had nothing to do with my personal needs even though staff believed it did.

On the other side, years of running services just like that leaves me with an uncomfortable awareness of doing that to others. Being compelled to adopt an authoritarian role which I sometimes like and often dislike. Telling people what to do. In my role as a professional, I ration limited resources and promote staff needs and desires, because they are usually more articulate and politically powerful. Unlike users, they belong to unions and professional associations.

I need to confront serious issues of racism, sexism and disablism within me. That process is very painful and I often need help. Most structures I have worked in have been extremely sexist, racist and above all – disablist, because until recently people with disabilities have protested the least.

Part of every professional's training should be to confront disablism. My training further confirmed me in my disablist attitudes and the skills learnt, diagnosis/assessment/treatment/prescription occurred within a dessicating medical framework. Unconsciously, I imbibed from various settings that people with disabilities were second-class citizens. For example, Wertheimer's important study shows the large element of disablism in health and social services advertising for staff.[29]

We need to return to the basic skills of counselling, not to develop complex and technical psychotherapy programmes, but that we may learn and listen more simply and fully. Those skills, tragically nowadays becoming so white-coated and technicalised, can help us to learn more about and act more sensitively to the complex needs of others and the millions of different ways in which they are expressed.

Those skills consists not only of listening but of helping to clarify; to help frame stuttering questions; to inform; to summarise; to suggest possible actions. All that can extend out to a knowledge of existing community facilities; to know their entry points; to know about structures and how to make them more consumer sensitive.

All of us, as doctors, psychologists, social workers, nurses, occupational therapists, boldly claim to pursue userist ends. 'The patient, client/resident/consumer comes first in this profession.' All of us know in our hearts that is untrue. We know it from our stay as patients in hospitals; from the experiences of our elderly relatives. Users are usually last in the queue. They don't ever have reserved car park places. No one really wants it that way. We are all userists now but there are just too many meetings, too many vested interests which stand between good intentions and good effects.

We will need completely new forms of professionalism in our diligent pursuit of normalisation. That must be more feminist in structure and operation. It will increasingly seek more cooperation and equity. We need to move towards new values, towards mutually humanising and liberating practices, rather than the traditional ignorance. It is essential to model and communicate the value and goodness inherent in ordinary human relationships.

We need new skills involving softer and more vulnerable parts of ourselves, less controlled and controlling, less manipulative and more loving. It means turning aside from the traditional hard shell of the paid worker. These new people will need substantial support and warmth to avoid the worst aspects of traumas.

We need increased flexibility based on the nature and needs of particular persons rather than on some generalised prescription for so called client groups. Person feeling rather than group think. General prescriptions are of limited help and techniques can be inherently dangerous.

We need more softness and gentleness to see who is really there. Our brothers and sisters everywhere suffer in poverty. Close contact can lead us naturally towards anger and indignation rather than to control. We must avoid further oppressing our own brothers and sisters.

## References

1. McCord, W., 'From Theory to Reality: Obstacles to the Implementation of the Normalisation Principle in Human Services', *Mental Retardation*, vol. 20, no. 6, 1983, p. 248.

2. Titmus, R., *Essays on the Welfare State* (London: Allen & Unwin, 1958) p. 125.

3. Brandon, S. 'Call for Revamping of CPN Role', *Nursing Times*, 29 March 1989.

4. Wolfensberger, W. (ed.), *The Principle of Normalisation* (Toronto: National Institute on Mental Retardation, 1972) p. 153.

5. Halifax, J., *Shaman— the Wounded Healer* (London: Thames & Hudson, 1982).

6. Ryan, J. and Thomas, F., *The Politics of Mental Handicap* (London: Pelican, 1980) p. 33.

7. Menzies Lyth I., *Containing Anxiety in Institution* (London: Free Association Books, 1988).

8. Timms, R. and Timms, N. *Perspectives in Social Work* (London: Routledge & Kegan Paul, 1978) p. 87.

9. Anderson, D. *Social Work and Mental Handicap* (London: Macmillan, 1982) p. 10.

10. Department of Health and Social Security, *Helping Mental Handicapped People in Hospital* (London: HMSO, 1982).

11. Pilgrim, D. (ed.), *Psychology and Psychotherapy: Current Trends and Issues* (London: Routledge & Kegan Paul, 1983) p. 1.

12. Roos, P., 'Behaviour Modification Procedures with the Normalisation Principle', see 4 above, p. 139.

13. Nightingale, F., *Notes on Nursing* (London: Constable, 1859).

14. Powell, E., *Medicine and Politics: 1975 and After* (London: Michael Joseph, 1982).

15. Bannister, D., 'The Internal Politics of Psychotherapy', see 11 above.

16. Olshansky, S., 'Vocational Behaviour through Normalisation', see 4 above, p. 153.

17. Brandon, A. and Brandon, D., *Putting People First* (London: Good Impressions, 1988).

18. Field, D., 'Emotional Involvement with the Dying in a Coronary Care Unit', *Nursing Times*, 29 March 1988, pp. 46–8.

19. Jones, M., *The Process of Change* (London: Routledge & Kegan Paul, 1982).

20. Chamberlin, J., *On Our Own* (London: Mind Publications, 1987).

21. Brandon, D. and Towe, N., *Free to Choose: An Introduction to Service Brokerage* (London: Good Impressions, 1989).

22. *National Symposium on Brokerage*, British Columbia, 1987.

23. Dyer, L., 'Lost Citizens', *Open Mind*, February – March, 1989.

24. Frost, B., 'Where Selecting Staff is a Joint Effort', *Social Work Today*, 13 October 1986.

25. Harper, G., 'Consumer-led Service Planning', *Community Living*, September 1988, p. 18.

26. McGee, J.J., *Gentle Teaching: A Non-aversive Approach to Helping Persons with Mental Retardation* (Nebraska: Human Sciences Press, 1987).

27. Flynn, R.J. and Nitsch, K.E., (ed.) *Normalisation, Social Integration and Community Services* (Baltimore: University Park Press, 1980).

28. Martin, A. and Parrott, R., 'Out on the Town', *Community Living*, vol. 2, no. 4, April 1989.

29. Wertheimer, A., 'Images by Appointment: A Review of Advertising for Staff in Services for People with Learning Difficulties', *Community Mental Handicap*, January 1988.

# Part II
# Experiencing Normalisation and Social Role Valorisation

# Introduction

This section of the book is devoted to the major contributors who create and participate in the experience of normalisation. In each of the four chapters the authors outline experiences in which they were personally involved, highlighting the intricacy of the issues entailed, indicating how much has been and still can be achieved. Yet this positive message does not obscure the difficulties or the doubts as to what is achievable and at what price.

It would be futile to attempt to rank the importance of the different constituencies or underestimate their interdependency. However, this interrelatedness is not of an equal magnitude, as discussed by Lawson (Chapter 3) and Segal (Chapter 4) in terms of the relationships between users and professionals, and by Lewis (Chapter 6) in relation to informal carers and planners. While Lawson and Warner (Chapter 5) demonstrate the possibilities and potential for the beneficial contribution of users to society and to the services system, Segal focuses on the vulnerabilities of the professionals in the encounter with disability and with people who suffer from it. Each of the authors also indicates the obstacles on the way to being socially valued, coming up with a list which only in part overlaps. The lack of overlap illustrates that in fact the various constituencies represent different perspectives, and that considerably more sharing would need to happen before a concentrated, joint effort towards the integration of people with disabilities could take place. In turn, ways and means by which it would be possible to overcome most of the identified change-blocking factors are explored.

While they all share the preference for achieving social role valorisation, Lawson expresses his doubts as to the value of reaching normalisation when this implies conformity to an unjust world – one we all know to be far from perfect. Moreover, he is suggesting that the disability entailed in mental distress is largely the creation of forces external to the person. Warner and Segal seem to take the existence of disabilities and their internal location for granted without necessarily refuting the central role of factors external to the person in worsening, generalising and perpetuating the impact of the disability, to the totality of the person's life. By pointing out that people diagnosed as suffering from schizophrenia in the Third World have a much better chance of leading a more ordinary life, Warner highlights in fact the potential contribution of the Western lifestyle and ethos to the fate of people with such a diagnosis in our

59

overdeveloped First World. Segal and Warner illustrate good practices of social role valorisation, if not integration, and how these can be creatively fostered even when risk-taking is involved (as invariably is the case). Lawson emphasises the value of users' mutual support. Segal focuses on the personal price paid by professionals for being emotionally involved in what happens to their clients, whereas Warner investigates the efficacy of a variety of different programmes to reduce and eventually resolve the separation of users from the rest of society. Touching on the issue of separate services run by users only, Lawson is suggesting that there is a positive role to be played by professionals within a system which gives pride of place to services run primarily by users. In fact the examples provided and the insight drawn by each of these authors demonstrate a high level of initiative and creativity, as well as genuine caring.

The discussion by Lewis in Chapter 6 of the processes of participation in parliamentary democracies complements the perspectives of users, professionals and managers, by focusing on a precondition for ensuring a dignified life for people with disabilities. Lewis offers a map of some of the most formidable obstacles to implementing any of the objectives of the new approach. The root of approaching people with disabilities as people first lies in the belief in the possibility of greater equality of opportunities and participation and the need to work towards it. Yet the considerable difficulties of participating in decision-making at any level by the majority of the population indicate how undemocratic our societies are in everyday life. She points out the urgency of ensuring the participation of ordinary citizens in decision-making, no less than that of direct and indirect service users. At the same time, the chapter contains examples which demonstrate that it is possible to stimulate a much greater measure of participation by policy-makers, those who care for a particular issue and of people directly affected by it than is usually the case, to the benefit of all. The more recent examples, such as the All Wales Strategy for people with mental handicap and Birmingham Community Care Action, give rise to cautious optimism for the future.

'And so the battle was staged between a crippled, sane boy and a hostile, sane, secretly savage though sometimes merciful world. Can I climb man-made mountains, questioned Josephy Meehan. Can I climb socially constructed barriers?'
Christopher Nolan, *Under the Eye of the Clock*

# 3
# A Recipient's View
*Mike Lawson*


**It's for your own good . . .**

It is for a variety of reasons, sometimes extremely complex, that an
individual finds her/himself at the receiving end of psychiatric
practices.[1]

It is assumed that the individual is somehow in need and that need
can be fulfilled. A whole range of labels thrown up by psychiatric
ideology can be bestowed upon the person, without any right of
reply by the recipient, or anyone else. The authority of the consultant
or 'expert' goes largely unquestioned.

For an overview of current service provision and the ideologies
that promote it five themes are particularly pertinent. Before any
agenda of benefit can be set we have to consider in more detail the
different approaches to madness and dissent through the centuries.
History reveals that behaviour perceived as deviant came to be
regarded as a medical rather than a spiritual or religious event with
the advent of the Industrial Revolution.[2]


## Magical/religious becomes rational/scientific

It is an awful irony that the notion of evil spirits was frequently dealt
with by use of the barbaric practice of trepanning, or drilling a hole
through the skull as a religious phenomenon to remove 'evil spirits'.[3]
Now, we do similar things — prefrontal lobotomy and electricity
being so-called 'scientific' treatments used by psychiatrists to treat
'mental illness'.[4]


## Personal responsibility versus uncontrollable forces

The inventors of the concept of 'schizophrenia', Kraepelin and
Bleuler, grouped together extremely diverse 'deviant' behaviours and
reduced them to a perception of symptoms of a disease.[5] When a
person is portrayed as not being responsible for breaking social
norms, s/he is then considered suitable for 'treatments'.

## The oppression of women

Sexism is not confined to psychiatry, although the notion of 'hysteria' being an identifiable 'illness' with a recommended 'treatment' of marriage, as well as Freud's fantasy about penis envy are but two examples of misogyny in the practice of ostensible medical beneficence.[7] Through feminism, we learn that it is preferable to reown and reassert some alternative ways of being in the world, rather than be seduced by valued but not necessarily valuable roles.[8]

## The overrepresentation of minority groups

Admission statistics in the UK reveal that Afro-Caribbeans are more likely to be admitted to 'mental institutions' than native born white people.[9] Especially revealing is the overrepresentation of Afro-Caribbeans as recipients of enforced incarceration under Section 136 of the Mental Health Act 1983, subsequent to police referrals.[10] Misdiagnosis and racial stereotyping have also been revealed by many studies.[11]

## Punitive and violent treatment towards people who are considered mad

A particularly ghastly example of punishment and ultimate violence is the connection between the Nazi holocaust and psychiatry.[12] The psychiatric profession was primarily responsible for inventing the concept of 'life devoid of value' and for putting the euthanasia programme into action.[13]

It is against that background that current services have evolved and emerged. We need to understand the political function of psychiatry before we can build appropriate quality services, and in this context we mean services that allow and encourage true and beneficial integration, by choice.

Often a recipient's view is dismissed by the 'mental health professional' as unscientific and anecdotal.[14] The dominant view put by the worker is seen as more valid because it is perceived as 'scientific'. Yet, life itself is a subjective experience and we all experience the world individually.

Admission into the institution has often been described as a 'degradation ceremony'.[15] It is easy to misunderstand the machinations of an individual's arrival when the question has been asked: 'What brought you in here?' Sometimes the most honest answer has been: 'An ambulance.'

In effect, to be a recipient of psychiatry is to walk a tightrope. One's behaviour had been adjudged suitable for psychiatric examination. The future of that individual is determined by the diagnostician. Therefore, effectively, to be diagnosed opens the door to the loss of personal autonomy and to disempowerment.

Traditionally, the individual is given a diagnostic label according to an arbitrary speculative interview, in which a particular lexicon is used.[16] One of the backbones of psychiatry was the invention of 'schizophrenia'. To quote Szasz:

> Schizophrenia has never been, is not now and probably never will be a bona fide medical diagnostic term . . . Psychiatrists do not know what schizophrenia is and don't know how to diagnose it . . . Schizophrenia has more to do with freedom and slavery than with health and disease . . . the ceaseless manufacture of disease names in psychiatry, together with a total lack of evidence for them – from agoraphobia to schizophrenia – is the greatest scientific scandal of our scientific age.[17]

The individual under scrutiny is already in an extremely vulnerable position. The diagnostician is employed to function in such a way as to discern what is believed to be some form of illness. It places the individual, who is often in a state of emotional turmoil, into a double bind. On one hand, there is clearly a reason for the individual to be in turmoil; on the other, the diagnostician is primarily there to make assessment. Not a good recipe for a useful relationship between recipient and the mental health profession.

However, useful relationships between recipients and professionals can occur when the professional is able to appreciate that:

1. the recipient is experiencing the consequence of cause and effect;
2. supportive allegiance and non-judgemental care is enabling;
3. 'Breakdown' can become breakthrough;
4. a political problem requires a political solution, i.e. to be poor, black, a woman, in a classist, racist, sexist society drives some of us to despair;
5. disempowering people drives some of us crazy;
6. individuals have individual reasons for distress and/or dissent.

The following is a useful example of what it feels like to be a patient, published by Rae Unzicker of the National Alliance of Mental patients in the USA.[18]

To be a mental patient is to be stigmatised, ostracised, socialised, patronised, psychiatrised.

To be a mental patient is to have everyone controlling your life but you. You are watched by your shrink, your social worker, your friends, your family. And then you are diagnosed as paranoid.

To be a mental patient is to live with the constant threat and possibility of being locked up at any time, for almost any reason.

To be a mental patient is to live on $86 a month in food stamps, which won't let you buy Kleenex to dry your tears. And to watch your shrink come back to his office from lunch, driving a Mercedes Benz.

To be a mental patient is to take drugs that dull your mind, deaden your senses, make you jitter and drool, and then you take more drugs to lessen the 'side effects'.

To be a mental patient is to apply for jobs and lie about how you have spent the last few months or years, because you have been in the hospital. And then you don't get the job anyway, because you have been a mental patient.

To be a mental patient is to watch TV and see shows about how violent and dangerous and dumb and incompetent and crazy you are.

To be a mental patient is not to matter.

To be a mental patient is to be a resident of a ghetto, surrounded by other mental patients who are as scared and hungry and bored and broke as you are.

To be a mental patient is to be a statistic.

To be a mental patient is to wear a label, a label that never goes away, a label that says little about what you are and even less about who you are.

To be a mental patient is never to say what you mean, but to sound like you mean what you say.

To be a mental patient is to tell your psychiatrist he is helping you, even if he is not.

To be a mental patient is to act glad when you are sad and calm when you are mad.

To be a mental patient is to participate in stupid groups that call themselves therapy. Music isn't music, it's therapy; volleyball isn't a sport, it's therapy; sewing is therapy; washing dishes is therapy. Even the air you breathe is therapy, and that's called 'the milieu'.

To be a mental patient is not to die — even if you want to — and not cry and not hurt and not be scared, and not be angry, and not be vulnerable, and not to laugh too loud . . . because if you do, you only prove that you are a mental patient, even if you are not.

And so you become a no-thing, in a no-world, and you are not.

In writing the above, in 1984, Rae Unzicker has said it all for millions of psychiatric 'patients' all over the world. Many of us feel the same way about our 'treatment' and the despair of our predicament, in which we are placed by others, which we see as a sanctioned social control apparatus.[19]

## Recipient's views on professional intervention

The majority of recipients, largely due to their distress, accept what is handed out, sometimes to the extent of being grateful. It is very difficult to see what is happening when one is in a state of emotional distress. The evidence that is emerging, such as the fact that in those areas where electricity (ECT) is not used, no more individuals per population commit suicide, is an alarming testimonial to the destructiveness and illogicality of psychiatry in practice.[20]

There is an awful danger in psychiatric 'research' that is sponsored by the pharmaceutical industry to promote the sale of chemicals with no real objectivity to their claims.[21] That was something illustrated through my relationship with a consultant psychiatrist who had been admitted while attempting to field trial a new neuroleptic drug on himself. He was indeed shocked at the contrast of his perception of being a recipient and actually becoming one.

It seems particularly pertinent that after the valuable experience of becoming a recipient he was never allowed to practise psychiatry again. Perhaps more alarming is the fact that the chemical he was dosing himself with had made him smash up his flat and attack a relative. That chemical is now widely prescribed. One myth of psychiatry is that the major tranquillisers caused a reduction in the inmate population of the institutions after their introduction in the 1950s. In fact the greatest reduction in populations was in the 1930s, due to policy change.[22]

The spectre of so-called side-effects and such manifestations as Tardive Dyskinesia, Tardive Psychosis and Dopamine Supersensitivity has raised awkward questions about the use of chemicals.[23] The assumption has been made that there is some parallel between diabetes and schizophrenia. Insulin can be measured but whatever chemical imbalance is supposed to cause 'schizophrenia' has not been discerned. Throughout psychiatry attempts to quantify it are regularly announced. Yet, to this day, no substantial or substantiating evidence has been found after endless research.[24]

## The way through the maze

What a grim picture that is of life as a psychiatric patient. But there are ways out of the maze and there are ways to change it all so that integration becomes an almost natural process. But first, a look at a specific attempt to make integration a valuable part of the process of re-empowerment. And a brief analysis of why, in my belief, it is insufficient.

In 1972, Wolfensberger stated that what we understand as 'mental illness' is 'largely, probably even always, caused or precipitated by interpersonal problems of living within the cultures.[25] He maintained this belief when he formulated the PASS system (Programme Analysis of Service Systems) as an evaluation tool of service provision, described in Chapter 2.

I had mixed feelings about the PASS course that I attended. A small number of us on the five-day programme were psychiatric system survivors. The majority were mental health professionals of varying ranks and disciplines. Without exception the recipients among us had a strong sense of outrage at the memory of our experiences in 'care'. I wondered if the service that we were to evaluate as part of the course would spread that outrage to the workers. The fifty delegates were divided into seven teams, each with a leader. It was strange to be working on the same side of the fence as the professionals and I felt a strong desire to run away. However, a sympathetic team leader and, particularly, an old friend from the self-advocacy organisation, Survivors Speak Out, made it possible and useful to stay.

PASS is described by its inventors as a method for the quantitative evaluation of human services. As a thermometer to evaluate services PASS is a valuable tool. As a service recipient I found the model useful and effective for the purpose of waking up professionals to the inappropriate nature of service facilities. It was useful for me to regain the sense of outrage at provision that recipients often feel. To have a dialogue with various professionals on the same level, rather than to submit to them as a higher authority, without the constant threat of their power to punish recipients was valuable. The equality of opportunity to exchange views and feelings just does not happen in the usual worker/recipient environments or relationships.

The major shortcoming, however accurate the evaluation, is that PASS is only a measure, rather than a remedy. The normalisation principle is based on 'the use of means which are valued in our society to as much as possible encourage and support behaviours, experiences and characteristics which are likewise valued'.[26] This is fine stuff if we as individuals benefit from the value system that we are heir to. Unfortunately, for some of us, the predominant value system is in itself unacceptable. The system of highly competitive profit-making ethos currently dominating the First World is not a desirable situation for many of us.[27] It therefore becomes paradoxical to equate the normalisation principle with decent living when the principle itself is bounded by an unacceptable political structure.

For those of us who see psychiatry as a form of covert social control, the PASS model is confined to an evaluation of acceptability within an unacceptable framework.

Presently in the UK, the mental hospitals are being run down and closed as part of government policy. As an evaluation tool, the model has a place as part of a package to facilitate integration as the closure process continues, subject to the reservations above.

For the recipient, there are a number of obstacles to surmount in the move from the institution back into the community. Not least are the geographical and environmental culture shocks. To live for a time in the physical dimensions of a hospital ward and then to move to a bedsit or flat or 'group home' can cause much distress, simply because of the contrasting space that one has access to. It takes some readjustment to adapt to sleeping alone after the communality of dormitory life.

My own experience of living in a 'mental hospital' created enormous difficulties upon release. It is still not appreciated sufficiently that there are two different worlds in operation and both have constraints, advantages and disadvantages relevant to the individual.[28] Within the institutions an automatic and spontaneous social life exists. Outside in the community it does not. I certainly felt alienated by the social requirements needed in order to meet other people outside the institution. It must be remembered that through being in the 'mental hospital' many of us lose contact with former friends and contacts outside. Upon release, one has to start all over again. And one feels powerless, demoralised, stigmatised, useless . . . However, it is possible to make the transition from institution to community easier with skills training for recipients and members of the community. Training is required for reconditioning to the frightening outside world. I forced myself to use public transport again. I felt a hero to use the London Underground because it was so alien an environment after the institution. We need training to make the readjustment to the difficult demands in the wider world, like social skills and assertiveness. Simple things like going to a restaurant for a meal can help an individual experience that it is possible to become integrated again.

Yet, going to a restaurant for the first time after one has been institutionalised is a terrifying experience. Many of us felt that we were visibly 'from the bin'. Training would involve gently testing the outside and reacclimatising.

The process of reintegration will be easier and more valuable according to the understanding not only of the validity but the *valuability* of the emerging individual. When the individual context of the person emerging is understood, then there is an opportunity to make the bridge.

The reintegration of individuals is currently largely determined by others who have power – the very hierarchy we distrust because of our hospital experience.

Various experiences of people leaving hospital show us that there is only one guaranteed way to regain our own power and therefore control over our own lives and ultimately true integration. That way is through *self-advocacy and self help.*[29] The only way to have a harmonious relationship with oneself and others is through self-respect. Advocacy and self-advocacy promote the growth of the individual and enable the process of valorisation; otherwise we are in submission or somehow perceived as inadequate. If disempowering individuals drives them crazy, then either not doing that or providing space for re-empowerment allows us all to lead potentially fulfilling lives. Power cannot be given, only advocacy and self-advocacy can ensure it is not taken away. Psychiatry is a sanctioned licence to remove power; self-advocacy and advocacy challenge and redress that imbalance. Power is essential to function and gain some autonomy and we regain our power through self-advocacy and advocacy.

This need not deny the mental health professionals a role. Workers can be redeployed as facilitators and supporters and indeed many have already been instrumental in the facilitation of self-advocacy initiatives in the United Kingdom. In this country we have a unique collaboration between recipients and ex-recipients and disaffected workers.

The American campaigner and survivor Judi Chamberlin, puts it well in the British edition of her book, *On Our Own*:

> From my distant vantage point, the British Survivors' movement appears to have some unique strengths. The ability of psychiatry's critics to come together, whether as system survivors or as radical workers, simply has not happened in the US or in any other country of which I am aware. If British activists can develop an ideology which combines the knowledge gained from both these viewpoints, respecting the different expertise of each, it will mark a major achievement in the struggle against psychiatric power. Both psychiatric survivors and radical mental health workers

propose an ideology of empowerment and autonomy; it remains to be seen if these two groups can overcome their historic differences, including class and power differentials, to promote these ideals for all.[30]

## Self-advocacy and re-empowerment

Although groups like the Mental Patients Union and People not Psychiatry have been around since the 1960s,[31] the significance of recipient participation in 'mental health' services is only just beginning to be recognised in Britain. The 1980s has seen a gradual emergence of recipient advocacy groups locally and nationally.[32]

As we move into the 1990s, there are thirty or forty local groups of various kinds (some simply supportive, some campaigning, some a combination) of patients' councils in various cities and towns, national self-advocacy groups and a 'Consumer Network' of several hundred within National MIND. These groups come together for important reasons. It is particularly difficult as a recipient of psychiatry to find the energy for such enterprises. With little money or resources, the enormity of need prompts us to do something about our distress given the inappropriateness of the existing psychiatric system. Dispossessed and chemically damaged individuals do not have the resources that are generally available for such activity.

Advocacy refers to the process of pleading the cause or acting on behalf of another person or persons to secure the services they require and/or rights to which they are entitled. Self-advocacy is where an individual seeks to represent their own concerns and interests. *Collective self-advocacy* is when a group of individuals seek to represent specific concerns and interests which they identify jointly. Legal advocacy or professional 'patient' advocacy is the term used to describe the broad range of methods and activities by which lawyers or other trained persons assist an individual to defend her/his rights.

The concept of advocacy in its present form was first developed in the United States and Europe in relation to 'mental handicap'. Holland was the origin of advocacy and patients' councils in the field of 'mental health'.[33]

The catalysis of our friends from Holland led to the formation of the national self-advocacy group, in the wake of the 1985 WFMH congress in Brighton. Nottingham was the first city in the UK to have established patients' councils in the hospitals (NPCSG). Funded by the local Social Services, the participants are all ex-inmates of the institutions with first-hand experience from the recipient perspective. The first core project team made an evaluation of opportunities for recipients to 'have any say in life on a hospital ward'. It was, of course, found that there were very few such opportunities.

The group's specific aims and objectives are:

1.  to create more awareness and control by users of the services we receive;
2.  to create user-only (Patients' Council) meetings in wards, day centres and community health centres and support such groups in taking up issues with staff and management;
3.  to influence the planning and management of mental health services;
4.  to educate workers, both locally and nationally, about the need for user involvement.

The NPCSG stresses that it is not the Patients' Council. The group exists to *support* patients' councils. 'We are not there to speak for users, but to support them in speaking for themselves. We are not there to criticise staff but to help users speak out for a better service. Often, users and staff want the same things!'[34]

Nottingham Advocacy Group (NAG) was set up two years later, with both groups increasing the input of users' views and supporting users to express their opinion. According to Nottingham Social Services, the policy of 'Daddy knows best' wherein all powers and decision-making is vested in professional interests, is increasingly coming into question. 'Importantly, this need is not just felt by patients; staff too are seeking new and better ways of meeting needs as we leave behind the certainties of the past.'

At a time when the hospital closure programme locally is approaching a crucial stage, the need for self-advocacy becomes more acute. Only an effective user voice can ensure that the new services which are developed to replace the old are more sensitive to users' wishes and needs, and that the process of transition has as few casualties as possible. An effective user voice is a voice that is heard, respected and acted upon. Like an effective statement, it is qualified with action that ensues, to the satisfaction of the person(s) who issue it.

I use the Nottingham example to illustrate the value of advocacy and self-advocacy with no apologises. Although still only a few years old, it is one of the longest running such initiatives in the UK and as such, is one of the most comprehensive. To date the group has been instrumental in presenting the users' perspective in a day unit, a day resource centre, a home, to members on the Community Health Council and the city Council's working party on disabilities. The local Citizen Advocacy Coordinator sums it all up:

> Recognition, from many quarters, is now giving credence to the importance of developing a comprehensive support structure for advocacy in order that users of the psychiatric services in Nottingham can effectively have a say in the planning and implementation of service provision, care and treatment which directly affects them. Advocacy has already commanded an importance within the Disabled Persons Act of 1986, as well as in policy documents discussed and published by the Health Service and the Social Services Department. What NAG and NPCSG offer is a constructive and positive supporting role so that people are able to take up that option as a right to self-expression and determination as now defined by the statute book. (Speech made at a meeting.)

The Patients' Council Support Group will be working more in the community as the closure of the local hospital draws near. They will be working with the multidisciplinary sector teams. Evidence of their influence is clear. For example, there has already been user involvement in the interviewing for a number of posts in day units – including that for a new consultant psychiatrist!

Involvement in these kinds of groups all over the country is an empowering experience in itself. Many of us, just a few years ago, would not have dreamed that that would be possible. The setting up of groups, alternative facilities, campaigns, costs much energy, resolve and commitment. But through that process comes a power, an ability to be a valuable person in the community. This is something that cannot be imposed from above by professionals or anyone else. It has to come from those who are disempowered and it has to grow through their determination to succeed in their chosen endeavour. For some this will mean cutting out workers altogether and taking the rocky route to finding sufficient funds to do their work 'on their own'. One criticism levelled at the patients' councils and their support groups is that these processes are collaborative and not revolutionary – thus prompting only reform rather than real change. Militant and separatist groups such as the German Irren Offensive, based in Berlin, demand a complete dismantling of psychiatry and all its structures. Separatist groups such as this and the present day Campaign Against Psychiatric Oppression in the UK believe that patients' councils maintain oppressive regimes. A separatist has said: 'The patients' councils are like new shoes for concentration camp victims.' May be the inmates of concentration camps need new shoes too. However, not at the price of maintaining oppressive institutions.

One great importance of the advocacy models is that in essence they bring together separatists and reformists of all colours, although for some any form of compromise or delay is seen as a negation of our purpose. There is *always* an element of frustration involved with integration work for all concerned, if their efforts are sincere.

Nationally, self-advocacy tends to have a slightly different role. It is worth noting here that there is not a cohesive 'recipient view' of the psychiatric system and mental health services. Each recipient has a different view, based on their own individual experience. That is why this chapter is titled 'A Recipient's View'. It is also why throughout the chapter, I draw on as many other voices from users and ex-users as I can. We can only speak for ourselves.

It was on the basis that there are many different opinions of what is appropriate, or right, or good in 'mental health' services that Survivors Speak Out, an organisation of users and allies, was founded. SSO does not attempt to put forward a concensus view of service provision and requirements. Probably the only thing each and every member of the organisation would agree on is that everyone has the right to be heard, whatever their views.

Survivors Speak Out was established early in 1986 to promote awareness of the real possibility of recipient action and to improve personal contact and the flow of information between individuals and groups. The organisation has a 'single-minded' approach and works effectively to promote self-advocacy. It has not involved itself in anti-drugs or anti-ECT campaigns, but sticks to the premise that every recipient has a voice and has a right to be heard. While attempting to raise national awareness about the issues, SSO is not representative in any formal sense, nor does it intend to be.

Peter Campbell, SSO secretary, writes: 'The roots of self-advocacy remain in the local areas and in locally based priorities.' He adds:

> After decades of being told that we can think nothing, do nothing, be nothing except a considerable burden to everyone else, we are actually doing some things for which we may soon be thanked.
>
> It remains important to remember that the objectives of mental health self-advocacy include changing the situation where the right to work, to vote, to be greeted as an adult are significantly denied people who have at some point ended up on the wrong side of a psychiatric medication trolley.[35]

As our Dutch colleagues have catalysed activity here in the UK, so the UK movement has its followers elsewhere. There is new direction on the Italian scene following visits to this country by allies from northern Italy. There, professionals are working towards ways in which recipients can be empowered to take control of their own lives again.[36] Recently, some of them have recognised that self-advocacy is really the only way to true integration.

For those of us who believe psychiatry is a form of social control the idea of democratic psychiatry is a contradiction in terms. However, the Psichiatria Democratica group led to substantial reforms in Italy. Law 180, some ten years ago, initiated the closure of all big 'mental hospitals'. Psichiatria Democratica as a group was composed of professionals and inspired the beginnings of a cultural integration.

Yet, ten years after the reforms of Law 180 there appears to be virtually no self-advocacy in Italy. Ironically, one of the reasons for this lack of recipient voices is the positive contribution of Psychiatria Democratica. To a certain extent it has been felt that there is no need for self-advocacy.

## Further horizons

As previously stated, the collaboration between recipients and some workers in the UK is unique. There is no doubt that workers have helped the self-advocacy movement in this country to establish and continue to work in all kinds of settings. It is obvious that where we can work together we should. There are, however, many examples of self-advocacy work in other countries which are of interest to illustrate further the point that this really is the only guaranteed way to re-empowerment and integration, whether facilitated by workers or not.

In the United States user-only initiatives have also proved that self-help is the best way forward. In her book, *On Our Own*, Judi Chamberline writes:

> There is much that must be done in order to build a system of viable alternatives. It is not a job that can be turned over to the 'experts', who have already failed. It is a task that must be done by all of us, ordinary citizens, working together. Those of us who are ex-patients have a vital role to play, since we know first-hand the inner workings of the present system and how it differs from the face it presents to the world.

By experiencing consciousness raising together, we can learn to see clearly the ways in which the psychiatric system has damaged us and the kinds of services that will provide true alternatives to paternalism and oppression. By working together to build alternatives that truly serve our needs, former patients can help ourselves and one another to grow strong.[37]

She continues:

Community has become an important word in psychiatry. 'Community' mental health centres have been established around the country and many professionals now call themselves 'community' psychiatrists. But the typical community mental health centre is no more a part of the community in which it is built than is the typical state hospital. Most community mental health centres are run by psychiatrists, or other mental health professionals, chosen by a state bureaucracy, who follow policies established by that bureaucracy . . . No real community is created, just the same old hierarchies. If this is to become the 'alternative' to mental hospital, nothing essential will have changed.[38]

An example of the kind of true 'alternative' that she writes about is the Ruby Rogers Centre in Boston, in which she is involved. Described as an advocacy and drop in, the centre is a place for self-help, socialising and advocacy. There is free membership to ex-patients, current patients, and people at risk of psychiatric incarceration. The centre is run by the membership and all decisions, forthcoming events and activities are discussed and voted on democratically at weekly business meetings.

The centre offers a number of groups on topics such as self-help, nutrition, art and music. Groups are run by members and suggestions for new ones are welcome. The centre literature states: 'We believe that every individual has the right to self-determination, and we oppose all forms of forced psychiatric treatment. We encourage our members to become knowledgeable about psychiatric drugs and other treatments, legal rights and other information that will help each person to make his or her own decisions on these important matters.' Members are women and men of all ages. They differ in many ways, but share the belief that through self-help and mutual support they can improve their lives. When examining these facilities workers often ask: 'But what do you do if someone is in crisis?' The answer is to regard the person in crisis as an individual with individual needs.

In an environment that feels safe, it is usually possible to ask the person in crisis what would be useful to them. Certainly, humanism and love go a long way. Very often, all people require is to not be interfered with and to be listened to, so that their requests have some value.

In the UK, with 90 per cent of state mental health funding still going into hospitals and only 10 per cent reaching community statutory facilities,[39] what hope does that leave for British recipient groups who wish to set up and run alternatives on their own terms? Not a lot. But somehow, with minimal resources, we manage. In Nottingham, many of those who work with NAG and NPCSG are volunteers; all those involved with Survivors Speak Out work in a voluntary capacity, and all the work done so far by that organisation has been achieved on a shoe-string budget with a few small grants and self-financing projects. The same is true of the scores of other groups and user-run alternatives throughout this country, and probably the world.

Let us stay in America for another example of self-help initiatives that genuinely re-empower the powerless and as far as integration is concerned provide more evidence that advocacy truly works. The Oakland Independence Support Center in California is a client-run facility for the homeless. It is a place 'for the homeless and those who are at risk of becoming homeless'. The centre is run by and for those who use it – the clients. Through planning meetings, committees and a representative community board, clients of the programme have full control over how the programme is run. The centre particularly serves people with 'mental disabilities' and former psychiatric patients. The major purposes of the centre are to assist people in obtaining an income, to find housing and provide support and skill to help prevent them from becoming homeless again.

It all started in 1981, when a group of mental health service recipients organised the Alameda County Mental Health 'Consumers Speak' Conference. The major message of that event was that recipients needed more rights and self-help programmes to meet their basic needs. One outcome was the forming of the Alameda County Network of Mental Health Clients. Since most of its members had been or currently were homeless, issues relating to homelessness, housing and financial benefits became a priority.

As the numbers of homeless people continued to grow, it became more and more evident that a large number had been in mental hospitals. Additionally, it was understood that being homeless itself caused severe stress related and emotional problems. 'Most homeless people,' states the Oakland Independence Support Center leaflet, 'have been mistreated by and therefore distrust the mental health system, Government agencies and traditional programmes. In order to maintain their independence they will not use these programmes and agencies.'

The OISC philosophy is basically that of self-help. The homeless, disabled and former patients can help themselves and each other. People who have experienced homelessness at first hand have an understanding and awareness that can only be gained from hard experience and thus are ideally suited to help others with similar problems. 'People who have been, but are no longer homeless, bring hope to others that their lives can improve as well.' The literature further stress: 'The homeless are very independent people and will maintain their freedom against all odds. Our philosophy is to support this and help people to maintain their independence, their human and civil rights. We believe that people have the right to have full control over the services that help them, and that all services be completely voluntary.'

In practical terms, the centre offers a place to drop in, socialise and make new friends. There is free food, support groups and other activities in a place that is supportive and safe. It offers a mailing address, use of bathroom and shower facilities, information and referral for food, shelter and other needed services. There is assistance for social services and financial benefits claimants. There is housing search assistance to find secure, decent and affordable housing. There is peer counselling, which is informal one to one counselling provided by other clients. There is money management assistance, independent living skills training and outreach to other programmes serving the homeless, assisting them to best help people with experience of the psychiatric system.

We need more of these kinds of services in every city and town if we are truly to begin to achieve integration with the community around us.


## The road to quality

Of course, there is a place for workers in all this. As previously stated, mental health professionals have played an important role in helping to set up and resource self-help and self-advocacy groups and schemes, and they will continue to do so. We need to work together, not in isolation from each other, towards ensuring the quality of services.

A definition of quality of service may be summarised as follows:[40]

1. Benefit to recipients, as defined by those recipients.
2. Responsiveness to the needs of recipients, as defined by recipients.
3. Effect of the service to add to the quality of life of its recipients, to the extent that they would feel as users, rather than used.
4. A service that any individual would find desirable and involving.

The fact that service users are probably less homogeneous than service providers at any given location indicates that service quality, as a degree of excellence, requires some fundamental upheavals and radical change.

My own experience as a service recipient and provider has illustrated the need for some basic precepts, as follows:

— Medicalising emotional distress or dissent obscures the issues and disempowers individuals.

— Individual and individualised strategies make for valid service provision.

— Professionals should be on tap not on top.

— Choices must be offered and resourced so that the recipient is enabled to be the main arbiter of service provision.

— Service provision must be culturally appropriate to the recipient. (This is particularly pertinent to ethnic minorities as they are substantially overrepresented in psychiatric institution.)

— A variety of alternative provisions radically different from present facilities must be made available.

— A public education programme to raise consciousness about the myths and negative stereotypes must urgently be put into action.

Emotional distress and dissent are products of sexism, racism, classism, competitiveness and the notion of the 'official version of reality'.[41] From this awareness, with management and control by recipients of alternative services and the demystification of dissent and distress, we can collectively produce service quality. Ultimately, for those of us who believe that psychiatry is a covert form of social control, the alternatives to promote understanding and support with new attitudes and destigmatisation with provide the philosophy whereby appropriate quality services will be built and resourced as a benefit to all, enabling everyone to enjoy a better life. Perhaps the only real measure of service quality is the extent to which that service encompasses and facilitates its recipients to increase the quality of their own lives on their own terms in their own chosen way.

Integrating recipients of institutional psychiatry into the world at large is rather like going from the frying pan into the fire. The black civil rights movement and the feminists have shown that we live in ways that lead people into dissent and distress.[42] The actual process of consciousness raising and subsequent re-evaluation of society will change the very society that drove us crazy in the first place. We are not being reintegrated into a static set-up. Society continually changes. Our integration will change society, simply by the fact that we are there. But if we are there with voices that are heard, the opportunity for change is great. And our valuability becomes more widely understood. There are numerous recipients throughout the world who are committed to changing the old precepts. Reintegration does not mean to us taking on the values of the existing society. It means being able to function within that society. It means being able to function within that society, having a voice there, being heard and being able to work for change without persecution. The emphasis is shifting to an understanding that we must change how we live, rather than 'treat' individuals who respond to oppression by behaving in ways that some may find difficult to understand. The focus is moving to the political systems that oppress us rather than the individuals who respond to that oppression in ways that are seen as 'sick'.

## Conclusions

Psychiatry, psychotherapy and psychoanalysis are born out of an assumption that certain individuals are disfunctionate and that the individual may at best be somehow cured or at least stabilised into 'normal', integrated behaviour with calculated intervention. To realise that it is not possible to intervene with the *individual* to achieve benefit requires a revolutionary change in attitude and perception. It is the *context* within which the individual exits that actually causes the reactions that are in turn perceived as deviance or 'mental illness'.

The first requirement for successful integration is a change in attitude. My own liberation from emotional distress, diagnosed as 'schizophrenia' and 'manic depression', originated from an awareness that I was not in fact 'ill' and never had been. That is not easy after being damaged and enraged by the system that promised to help me. That awareness enabled me not only to stay out of the institution, but to stop taking the chemicals that I had been told I would have to take for the rest of my life. It was not simply a grudging dissent, it was an awakening to the relationship between cause and effect in my life. That understanding was delayed many years due to the confusing effects of my initial distress and the 'treatment' which followed, which was a compound of various coercions.

To endure the indescribable agony and distress and then experience the humiliations of incarceration, chemical poisoning and electrocution is more than any human being can be expected to bear. To make sense, through this oppression, of one's reasons for dissent and/or distress is a gargantuan task. My 'diagnosis' was made out of context with my life history, my behaviour was judged, but the reasons for it were never understood by the consultant. This experience is by no means unique. Many recipients share these conclusions.[43]

For integration to work, it is necessary to understand the errors that caused the misunderstandings, leading to the dominance of psychiatric intervention. Marginalised groups in our communities are overrepresented in the institutions.[44] Some would argue that they experience more 'mental illness' because of their plight and disadvantage. Certainly, to be marginalised is distressing and individuals will respond to oppression in an oppressed way. That is not a 'mental illness', or even a 'mental health problem', it is a valid response! It is easier to find fault with an individual who is expressly dissent and/or distress than it is to look critically at the society which causes it. Political systems based on inequality, the confines of the nuclear family and class systems actually need social control systems to function. When the elite minority is exploiting the majority, psychiatry fulfils this purpose.[45]

To achieve integration, we must change the way we relate to each other and create appropriate multilayered support systems and a redeployment of resources. The 'dis-integration' resulting in the creation of the 'mental patient' fulfilled a basic requirement of the political regimes that created them.[46]

Furthermore, it must be appreciated that psychiatrised individuals have experienced an oppression that requires remedy in the form of effective deinstitutionalisation. Many of us experienced substantial damage, both emotionally and physically, from the very means that were ostensibly supposed to alleviate our distress.[47]

Self-help and self-advocacy are the only way to provide appropriate services. We all need the same things – decent homes, valued occupation, friends, enough money, opportunities, choices, options.

Whether we are labelled 'ill' or as 'successful professionals' we all need the same – to be valued, valuable, to have the opportunity to be special. And we all need this on our own terms. As a recipient stated: 'We know we are right because our experience has taught us that psychiatry is wrong and we will win the battle as they themselves also begin to realise it.'

The journey towards the reintegration of individuals deemed 'mentally ill' is well under way. Yet we need a new awareness, the redeployment of resources and the opportunity to facilitate, run and manage a wide spectrum of structures based on local need, so that services are based on the needs of recipients, as those recipients define them. As we succeed, everyone benefits and our communities become enriched with this new investment.

Lastly, from a friend at the Oakland, USA, centre for the homeless, Howie T. Harp, a pertinent question for everyone: 'If you are in a position to help people in crisis, ask yourself *why*? The answer can be most illuminating!'

# References

1. McCormick. E.W., *Nervous Breakdown* (London: Unwin Paperbacks, 1988).
2. Hill, D., *The Politics of Schizophrenia* (Philadelphia: University Press of America, 1983).
3. Masson, J.'M., *A Dark Science: Women, Sexuality and Psychiatry in the 19th Century* (New York: Collins, 1986).
4. Stafford-Clarke, D., *Psychiatry Today* (London: Pelican, 1952).
5. See 2 above.
6. Cochrane, R., *The Social Creation of Mental Illness* (London: Longman, 1983).
7. See 2 above.
8. Brown, H. and Smith, H., *Feminism and its Lessons for Community Care* (London: King's Fund, 1988).

9. Mercer, K., 'Racism and Transcultural Psychiatry', in Miller, P. and Rose, N. (eds), *The Power of Psychiatry* (Oxford, Polity Press, 1986).

10. Rogers, A. and Faulkner, A., *A Place of Safety* (London: MIND, 1987).

11. See 9 above, and Shasidharan, S.P., 'Towards an Anti-racist Psychiatry', paper given at the conference: Black Perspectives on Mental Health Care, London, November 1988.

12. Masson, J., *Against Therapy* (London: Collins, 1989).

13. See 2 above.

14. Rosenham, D.L., 'On Being Sane in Insane Places', *Science*, 250–8.

15. Goffman, E., *Asylums* (London: Pelican, 1961).

16. American Psychiatric Association, *Diagnostic and Statistical Manual of Mental Disorders (DSMIIIR)* (Washington DC, 1987).

17. Szasz, T., *Schizophrenia, the Sacred Symbol of Psychiatry* (New York: Basic Books, 1976).

18. As quoted in Burstow, B. and Weitz, D. (eds) *Shrink Resistant* (Vancouver: New Star Books, 1988).

19. Ibid. 18.

20. Warner, R., *Recovery from Schizophrenia* (London: Routledge & Kegan Paul, 1985).

21. Socialist Health Association, *Goodby to All That?* (London, 1987).

22. See 20 above.

23. Breggin, Dr P.R. *Psychiatric Drugs: Hazards to the Brain* (New York: Springer Publishing, 1983).

24. See 21 above.

25. Wolfensberger, W. (ed.), *The Principle of Normalisation in Human Services* (Toronto: National Institute on Mental Retardation 1972).

26. Wolfensberger, W. and Glenn, L., *PASS – Programme Analysis of Service Systems*, 3rd ed (Toronto: National Institute on Mental Retardation, 1975).

27. See 20 above.

28. See 15 above.

29. Barker, I. and Peck, E. (eds), *Power in Strange Places* (London: Good Practices in Mental Health, 1987).

30. Chamberlin, Judi, *On Our Own* (London: MIND, 1988). Similar views are expressed also in: Zinman, S., Howie, T. Harp, and Budd, S., *Reaching Across: Mental Health Clients Helping Each Other* (Boston: California Network of Mental Health Clients, Centre for Psychiatric Rehabilitation, Boston University, 1987).

31. Barnett, M., *People not Psychiatry* (London: Allen & Unwin, 1973).

32. See 29 above.

33. Van de Graaf, W. and Wiegand, H., *The Dutch Model*, paper presented at the International Conference on Users Involvement in Mental Health Services, University of Sussex, 26–28 September 1988.

34. See 29 above.

35. Campbell, P., 'Users Power', in Barker and Peck, see 29 above.

36. Ramon, S. (ed.) *Psychiatry in Transition* (London: Pluto Press, 1988).

37. See 30 above.
38. Ibid.
39. *The Social Services Select Committee: Care of Adult Mentally Ill*, House of Commons, 1985.
40. Lawson, M. and Biggs, J. *Quality in Community Care*, paper presented to the World Federation of Mental Health, London, December 1988.
41. See 2 above.
42. See 8 above.
43. See 30 above.
44. See 6 above.
45. See 2 above.
46. Johnstone, L., *Users and Abusers of Psychiatry* (London: Routledge & Kegan Paul, 1989).
47. See 30 above.

'Together they would struggle, the boy blowing like a whale from the huge effort of trying to discipline his bedamned body. Every tip of his pointer to the keys of the typewriter sent his body sprawling backwards. Eva held his chin in her hands and waited for him to relax and tip another key. Young Boyblue honestly gave himself over to his typing teacher. Gumption was hers as she struggled to find a very voluntary tip coming to the typewriter keys from his yessing head.

Perhaps it won't happen for me today he teased himself but he was wrong, desperately, delightfully wrong. Sweetness of certainty sugared him now. Yes, he could type. He could freely hit the keys and he looked in the mirror and met her eyes . . . But for Eva Fitzpatrick he would never have broken free.'

Christopher Nolan, *Under the Eye of the Clock*

# 4
# The Professional Perspective

*Julia Segal*

In my experience, few professionals seem to have heard of the concept of 'normalisation' – and even less, the latest version: 'social role valorisation'.[1] On the other hand, it now seems to be taken for granted amongst many professionals that in principle, people with mental or physical disabilities should be treated 'just like anyone else'. There is an increasing recognition of the 'normal' or 'non-disabled' aspects of people and the importance of taking these aspects into account. There is an awareness of some of the devaluing attitudes and behaviour of professionals, of the undesirable consequences of this, and a desire to make sure that their own behaviour and attitudes are not disabling of others.

This chapter is not about 'normalisation' *as it should be*, but about these (far less radical) ideas which seem now to be held by many professionals, partly as a result of the work of those in more senior positions who have a more sophisticated view of normalisation. It looks at some of the issues which arise when professionals at all levels try to put *their own* awareness of the need for change into practice.

## Changes of attitude and belief

Professionals differ from the non-professional population in that they have been selected and trained to work in particular ways, socialised by their peers and required to abide by certain standards, stated or implicit. These standards change over time, so that earlier generations may have different expectations from later ones; the interaction in the workplace of staff from different generations may enhance or counter formal training. In order to produce change in professionals, then, there is a need for input not only at the level of initial training, but also in the workplace. The experience of older generations of staff must be accessed and used in such a way that it permits and encourages new ideas to be developed realistically and put into practice, rather than simply blocked.

85

Power relations are an important element of professionalism. Professionals act as gate-keepers for many services which have the potential to relieve many kinds of pain and suffering. Part of the changes required of professionals (and their clients) therefore involves renegotiating existing power relations: this is always a difficult task.

A further complication is the responsibility some professionals take, to contain and limit not only the physical but also the mental suffering of the people who come to them for help. Some, such as counsellors and some social workers, have been trained to hand responsibilities back to the client in a modified and bearable form.

Others, such as most doctors and nurses have been trained to see it as their responsibility to protect their patients from worry. Prolonged exposure to this kind of relationship with professionals not only denies patients access to information essential for exercise of control over their own bodies or lifestyles, but also may work to deskill and prevent the acquisition of skills essential for an independent adult life. Challenging such professional belief systems may be extremely threatening to the professionals concerned.

Amongst the more politically aware professional care staff, the meaning of caring has changed. Protective attitudes tend to be seen as patronising and as undermining the abilities and competence of the recipient. The very word 'patient' is rejected on the grounds that it defines someone simply by their (unsatisfactory) relation to the medical profession. Some of the distinctions between staff on the one hand and patients on the other are challenged and the syndrome of 'institutionalisation' is acknowledged. There is some agreement as to how one should not behave and think, but far less clarity about what kinds of behaviour or attitudes are desirable.

### Treating people 'normally'

By treating people in an 'ordinary' or 'normal' way, as distinct from treating them as 'patients' it is hoped that more normal behaviour and aspects of the personality will be encouraged. This view has both value and limitations.

> A group of people, moved out of institutions for 'the subnormal' into a sheltered housing scheme where they were allowed and enabled to look after themselves, changed enormously within the first year of living independently. People who had known them before the move said they would not have recognised them.

A boy with multiple handicaps was sitting silent and hunched up, openly masturbating. Nobody stopped him or considered doing anything about it because they did not expect anything different from boys 'like him'. When a psychotherapist began to work with him in the same way as she would have worked with anyone, not only did his masturbation stop, but his language and his posture also changed radically. He also began to protest about his lifestyle.

Attempting to treat people 'normally' raises immediate difficulties. What is normal? Who wants to be ordinary anyway? Psychotherapy itself offers a new kind of unequal, 'patient' role, but it may bring about the possibility of a far more 'normal' existence. Does the new culture demand a rejection of the safety and predictability of a clearly defined 'staff' role in an institution? Will this not expose the private individual? If staff are to show their feelings, what about the less popular people, be they clients or staff? If a bit of friendliness is shown, will 'they' not make huge, unsatisfiable demands? How should staff react to conflicting demands and conflicting standards of behaviour from each individual client and staff member?

'Normal' behaviour is not necessarily desirable or congruent with the professional beliefs held by staff groups. Depending on the subculture concerned, it may be normal to hit back or to call the police when people become violent; to shut mad people up in mental hospitals; to wrinkle the nose and express disgust at the smell of urine; to recoil from ugliness or even a minor deformity. It is also normal not to expect too much of people who are ill. And yet the theory may be understood to require that people who are behaving in a very abnormal way or making abnormal demands themselves, be it for reasons of mental or physical differences, be treated in a 'normal' way, while proscribing calling the police, mental hospitals, social rejection and cruelty. What kind of allowances are patronising and what kind should be made? In terms of social behaviour, once professionals begin to think about what they consider normal, it becomes evident that there is a huge variety of opinions. Staff in one institution had backgrounds which included a village in Ghana in the 1950s; the East African Asian community; Welsh Methodism in the 1940s; a Norwegian town in the 1980s; London (Jewish working class and atheist/Christian public school) in the 1960s; and two different Caribbean countries. In any institution, staff and clients may be drawn from different cultures or subcultures. In these circumstances it may be impossible to agree on definitions of 'normal' except to say that it is normal to disagree.

*Acceptable behaviour*

What in fact is required is that definitions of acceptable behaviour change; somehow people have to find ways of relating to each other which no longer demand that those with disabilities have to conform to a set of roles which have become unacceptable. In particular, professionals are having to discover new ways of giving more power over their own lives to clients, and ways of responding effectively when such power is demanded by the users of their services. They also have to find ways of helping to mobilise other supportive resources in the community.

> New flats for people in wheelchairs were built in such a way that there was no wheelchair access to the flats upstairs, and people in wheelchairs could only visit each other with great difficulty. The professional worker responsible for helping to settle in the residents had not noticed this omission. She saw 'support' as coming entirely from herself and the families of the people concerned; she had also not thought of the residents visiting her in her office, as other users of her services did. She had not considered that the residents should be able to go out and both seek their own support and give it to others.

The segregation of people with disabilities or any kind of difference from others, now seen as institutionalised rejection, has always been defended as a form of protection for a vulnerable group from the attacks and cruelty of the outside world. Patronising attitudes are part of an attempt to cover up hostility. Removing patronising behaviour may simply leave a more naked hostility. Removing special schools may simple leave children vulnerable to the bullying of 'normal' children.

The question raised is whether it is possible for society to handle the disturbing and rejecting feeling raised by disabilities in any other way than by removing the victim. At present it seems that there are two important courses of action. One is to become more aware of the hostility and attempt to understand it in order to change it. The other is to revise ideas about the ways people with disabilities can and should respond to the negative treatment they receive. We have to see them as at least potentially able to look after themselves socially, and perhaps ensure that they are allowed to or taught how to, even when this means that previous professional or administrative roles are turned upside down.

Whether we can simply get rid of negative reactions or not we do not yet know. Attitudes to people with low incomes, to women and to homosexuality as well as to people with disabilities have all changed over the last twenty years, but none of these changes has meant a total removal of negative reactions. Increased social contact with people who were previously marginalised can reduce some of the suspicion, fear and other negative feelings and attitudes towards them. However, the contact has to be pleasurable: in a school it has to be handled well, for example. If it is not, it may simply bring to the surface cruelty and rejection which will prove too strong for the social group to handle without damage to the already damaged individual with the disability. Some of the negative reactions of the general public, including professionals, are a response to low self-evaluation, self-rejection or other negative attitudes held by people with disabilities themselves. Bullies in the professions as elsewhere may pick on those who show themselves vulnerable. These attitudes need to be changed by the work of people with disabilities themselves, but professionals have a potentially two fold role as partners in this process. They can change those aspects of their own behaviour which reinforce or create negative attitudes towards people with disabilities, and they can also directly challenge these attitudes when they discover them in the people they work with.

The work of a counsellor, for example, by its nature should raise the self-esteem of the client.

It was Mrs Smith — she works at the Day Centre — who really made me feel I was a man and should apply for this job. (Man with disability who had obtained his first job for twenty years, working for an organisation fighting for disability rights.)

Professionals who wish to work as partners in this way may have to work hard to overcome rejection arising from the behaviour of their predecessors.

You can't trust the District Nurses: they never listen; they always think they know better. When I come back I always find his clothes have been put on wrong or something, and he's been really uncomfortable. It's not worth going out. (Woman whose husband needed personal care.)

Changes of attitude and belief and new ways of working always involve resistance and hard work. Depression may be a necessary part of the work involved, as anxieties which previously were avoided can no longer be dealt with in the same way and have to be confronted and suffered.[2] From an organisational point of view this may mean increased absenteeism and loss of staff. The uncertainty and upheaval caused may further lower morale.

New staff coming in to the service may or may not have more appropriate attitudes to the new task in hand. If rates of pay are low there may be an increase in less able workers. This poses new problems for in-service training. Unless both the competence and the self-confidence of the new staff is built up on a realistic basis, they are likely to undermine any attempts of clients to build their own self-confidence.

## Who needs training?

### Staff with different origins

'Normalisation' involves two quite separate situations. People who previously offered services mainly or exclusively to those without obvious disabilities may now be required to offer the same services to people with disabilities. For example, Relate Counsellors are being asked to counsel people with multiple sclerosis, and staff in adult education institutions (e.g. the City Literary Institute, London) are being asked to extend their programmes to provide for a new clientele including people with very low educational attainments.

At the same time, staff who previously worked with people with disabilities in institutions of one kind or another are being asked to change their place and/or methods of working. In this category are staff moving out of mental hospitals or mental handicap institutions to help develop new ways in which their ex-patients can live in the community.

These two groups face different anxieties and problems. Each has new and different requirements for training and support. Both have to unlearn previous attitudes arising from socialisation or training.

Further differences in terms of anxieties, expectations and training arise from the particular disability involved.

### Different client groups
Physical disabilities (including chronic illness), mental handicap and psychotic states of mind (i.e. mental states in which contact with reality is broken) all raise different issues for professional staff. To some extent this is a result of staff identifying with the client group concerned. Staff may be more or less vulnerable to the particular feelings aroused by the condition involved. Within these groups,

each specific disability interacts with the personality, history and other characteristics of the individuals concerned. This gives rise to different reactions in the person with the disability and in people around.

I want now to pick up some of the issues of particular relevance for staff attempting to implement new ideas about treating people in a more 'normal' way. In each case I will then consider some of the training implications.

*Denial*
Denial is common to all disabilities and to clients and professionals alike. Denial in one of its many forms is a natural initial response of hostility and rejection towards an unwanted situation. Although in the short term it may do little harm, or may even free the mind to concentrate on other important issues, in the long term consequences may be serious.

Denial is used in many different ways. It may be used against realistic *perception of disabilities themselves*. It is remarkably easy to overlook missing legs at times; the distortions of perception involved in psychoses may also be misinterpreted and ignored by staff. A child born with a disability may have to cope with parents who want to do away with the disability, but instead attempt to do away with their perception of it. An adult faced with a new disability may seek to deny the reality and consequences, just as they would for any serious, unwanted loss, for two years or more.

Denial also functions against *perception of emotional responses* towards the disability. Professionals forced to see the disability may attempt to ignore the person who has it, in the unconscious hope of avoiding the full impact of awareness of the emotions involved. Some people with disabilities manage their lives in such a way that they avoid becoming conscious of the emotions it gives rise to either in themselves or in others. Such people may exert strong pressure on staff to also overlook the disabilities involved, and staff may find themselves in a conflict, where they are being asked to ignore something they cannot ignore, by a person whose wishes they feel they should treat with respect. Maintaining an 'as if' relationship in which a disability is ignored creates strains on both sides which are difficult to confront, particularly since the professional may be unsure that they have the right to challenge a denial they may themselves consider to be adaptive.

This is quite different from the situation where emotional reactions to the disability can be experienced realistically and overcome, leaving the person with the disability able to use their capacities to the full. Staff relations with such people are likely to be far more relaxed; staff reactions to the disability can be handled better both by the staff themselves and by the person concerned. Both joking and serious comment on the effect of the disability may be possible.

Denial of emotional response is also sometimes evident in attitudes to children with serious intellectual difficulties. Adults often overlook the child's emotional capacities. The child is not expected to react in a normal way to events such as a death in the family. This may also explain the frequency of abuse of such children; there may be a feeling that 'what they don't understand cannot hurt them'. The damage done to the child is then compounded by the fact that no one takes its emotional reactions seriously, these being dismissed as normal for children 'like this'.

The difficulties for professionals here are considerable. Once they begin to look at the emotional state of such children or infantilised adults in their care, they may find themselves uncovering emotions which are quite devastating. Where the child or handicapped adult has been deprived of emotionally close relationships since an early age, they may use a new relationship with staff to externalise conflicts in the way a very demanding small child might. Staff may find themselves caught up in these conflicts, which are likely to be quite disturbing and to involve struggles with authority figures such as parents. It may be difficult for staff to make clear judgements about real-life events and the correct response to them. The strength of the emotional response may also frighten the staff member who may seek a way of withdrawing without losing face.

Patronising or pitying attitudes may cover hostility. So too may avoidance tactics. The consequences for work may be serious.

> A psychologist rang me to talk about a client he was seeing who had a chronic deteriorating paralysis. He said he felt very sorry for her. I asked if he felt this feeling came from him or was evoked by the client herself. There was a pause and the psychologist said 'actually, she makes me feel really angry, it's just that it doesn't seem fair when she has so much to cope with'.

Here the pity was a cover for a much more vigorous – and in the circumstances, more productive – group of emotions evoked in the professional. The psychologist was disabling himself by covering up his anger, which he needed to recognise in order to work with his client.

Valerie Sinason[3] has described vividly the 'idiot smile' used by adults towards children with deformities or with intellectual deficits and reflected by such children and adults. This is often accompanied by the phrase 'Are you all right?' which leaves no space for real communication of pain, sorrow or misery. She links this with the difficulty adults have in acknowledging their perception of the loss and mental pain involved in such disabilities. It may also cover a powerful hostility, and be perceived as such by the child or adult concerned. Pretence of unconcern and pretence of being 'all right' may be felt to be the only possibility for relationships.

Denial of disability in this case as in so many others, actively prevents the acknowledgement and recognition of realistic emotions of all kinds. Loss is denied and happiness is devalued by being falsified. Acknowledgement and recognition is essential for the development of realistic and mature relationships with the self and others in both adults and children, professionals and parents. It is important here to distinguish between the child's sense of loss and the professional's in imaginery identification with the disabled child. Where the professionals cannot handle their own grief they may see no further than the damaged and disabled aspects of the child. Training seems to be necessary before many professionals can begin to imagine how the world might really look from the point of view of someone who has been disabled from birth or a long time ago. It may be this which obstructs a more normal recognition of strengths and abilities, including the ability to enjoy life, in people with disabilities of any kind.

## Idealisation

Where the feeling associated with a disability are difficult to handle, people sometimes respond by idealising. They may idealise the disability or 'the disabled' or a particular person with a disability. 'You're so brave!' or 'Aren't you wonderful!' can make the recipient cringe as if they have been attacked, in a way that a more realistic recognition of their strengths will not.

A voluntary care worker who had MS for twenty-five years tells with delight how one day she discovered she did not have to like everyone with MS she met. She was talking to a woman who was infuriating her, and she suddenly realised she would have disliked her before she had MS and there was no reason for not disliking her now. This felt like a liberation.

Where, as in this case, the idealisation breaks, dislike may be perceived. This leaves the problem of distinguishing whether feelings of antagonism or discomfort are a result of disability, and therefore perhaps could and should be overcome in some way, or whether they are a result of socially acceptable personality clashes. In these circumstances, people often use as a yardstick the behaviour they feel they would show in the absence of a disability. This still leaves difficult problems: how do you behave 'normally' towards someone with an obvious deformity or disability?

### How do you behave 'normally' towards someone with an obvious deformity or disability?

This problem effectively prevents some professionals offering their services to people with disabilities. There can be a fear of doing the wrong thing; most people have no experience of handling the problem of when, whether or how to offer assistance, for example, with walking, with pushing a wheelchair, or taking off a coat. They may fear the humiliation and confusion of being in an unfamiliar situation with no previous experience to help them. Many people fear insulting or offending; they fear accusations of being patronising or thoughtless; they may also fear the consequences of drawing attention to a disability felt as unmentionable.

There is often no idea that people with disabilities themselves may have both the means and the willingness to help in these situations. It seems that part of the normal way of looking at people with disabilities involves assuming that their minds are a blank, or at the very least, quite different from other people's. Even when this attitude is felt to be wrong, it is still found in automatic assumptions which have to be individually discovered and challenged. Where there is an unspoken communication of massive denial of some aspect of the disability by either party, there is real difficulty in the two people concerned joining forces to overcome any embarrassment of social awkwardness involved.

It is important to note that none of these issues has been routinely addressed in training for professionals. Working with people with non-acute disabilities may have been seen as only a small part of the wider load, and insufficient time devoted to it on any professional curriculum. The training and socialisation of doctors in particular has until recently been notable for its failure to address the problem of handling relationships with any patients, disabled or able bodied. Training remains largely dominated by senior doctors who are themselves untrained in interpersonal skills. They are in a position to resist strongly any implication that their own skills are inadequate, and so prevent change. Defensiveness and insecurity in this area then contributes to the difficulties doctors have, both in treating patients of all kinds with respect, and in seeking help in learning new ways of behaving towards them.

Part of the difficulty lies in the fact that people respond to the injunction to 'treat people normally' as if it could only involve denial of the disability. This is where the measurement against behaviour in the absence of a disability comes in; the assumption is that it is possible to ignore the disability and to react as if it were not there. Unfortunately, this is often not possible; by definition, disabilities have some disabling effect on someone, be it the person who 'has' it or those around. (Serious speech defects, for example, may disable the listener as much as the speaker; so may feelings of great pity; or inhibitions arising from childhood injunctions such as 'don't stare!').

It is really difficulty to speak angrily adult-to-adult to an adult who is very much smaller and weaker. I was invited to speak at a day course on MS run by a disability association. The organisation was disastrous, and specific requests I had made were ignored. Afterwards I did not reassure the organiser when she apologised for the waste of my and my colleagues' time, but showed that I was annoyed about it. This took a conscious effort owing to the fact that the person concerned was in a wheelchair and very much smaller than me. I went away unsure if I had behaved reasonably or not. I reminded myself of a previous occasion where I had expressed similar feelings to someone who was not only not disabled, but also in a position of power over my job; this reassured me, but not wholly.

Afterwards, I wondered how many times the organisers concerned had been kept waiting by professionals such as myself and my colleagues, who included a doctor and physiotherapist. I wondered how often they had felt they could not complain, and if there had been some sense of getting their own back on us, or putting us in our place by keeping us waiting. If so, I felt there might have been some reason for keeping us waiting, but I did not think it was much of an excuse. I also wondered if I was just trying to show that I was not intimidated by the wheelchair and the rather motherly person in it. This kind of tangled soul-searching is not unusual amongst professionals who want to behave correctly in a new situation, and are unsure of the rules.

Normal behaviour may depend on evoking a normal response. It is normal for adults to use play fights or physical restraint with children as a way of communicating both affection and power relations.

Where the child is very weak, the experience and its significance for adult and child is very different. The adult has to handle the perception of the child's weakness, and the pain of this. The child has to handle the adult's pain, whether the child feels the loss of muscle power or not. The child may be left having to handle being avoided by an adult who does not want the hurt of such an interaction.

### Conflicts between people with obvious disabilities and people without

These are likely to arise in some form in any interaction between people with disabilities and people apparently without. These external conflicts may represent conflicts within the self between parts seen as 'disabled' and parts seen as 'not disabled', in whatever sense. Neither party in this case will see the other as a real person. Here I would like to look at some of the conflicts which affect professionals attempting to behave 'normally' with people with disabilities.

Rejection seems to be an almost universal initial response to imperfection. (Adolescents' anxieties about their own imperfect bodies demonstrate how widespread this is.)

People feel bad about rejecting others and may avoid them to prevent awareness of this feeling . . .

There is a problem in that other people's helplessness or dependence upon us leaves us with a greater responsibility for keeping in check our own cruel and sadistic impulses. It seems we have reason to fear misusing our power over people who are dependent upon us. This is true for anyone. Staff whose own self-confidence is weak, and who have been ill-treated in their own past, victims of abuse of any kind as children or adults, are especially vulnerable to evoking feelings of victimisation in those in their care. This is a particular tragedy for those staff who have entered the caring professions in order to care for people seen as representing the helpless, dependent aspects of themselves.[4]

Where staff feel supported themselves, they may be better able to support and care for their clients. Where they feel undermined or undersupported by the employing hierarchy, they may undermine or fail to support clients. This reflection process can also work in the other direction. Where staff feel undermined and attacked by clients – as is common for staff working with ex-mental patients, for example – they may undermine and attack the hierarchy, often provoking retaliation.

There are many conflicts between people with disabilities and those who assist them in one way or another. It is not at all easy to relate to someone who comes in to help with tasks which the person concerned would like to be able to do for themselves. A mother who cannot look after her baby without help from outside; a woman who cannot wash or dress herself; a man who cannot shave himself may all make life unpleasant for those who come to offer 'community care'. Where this care is offered at home rather than in an institution the role of the professional carer may be made harder. The support of other staff is missing, and so too is the distraction from observing the emotional state of the person concerned. The closeness may be painful to live with.

A young woman working as a Personal Care Assistant for three women who had moved out of a long-stay hospital said how awful it was to be alone for eighteen hours at a stretch. She meant she was alone except for the three women. It seemed that the sense of isolation might have been partly a reflection of the isolation felt by these women. They had never lived anywhere other than in an institution and did not seem to have friends or to like each other. They had agreed to live together to get out of the hospital, rather than out of a choice of flat-mates. In the hospital they had only related to nurses, who came and went. One said she and her mother hated disabled people; this included her flat-mates, and she did not want to associate herself with them.

The attempt to create more normal living arrangements for these women had brought the professionals involved up against a new appreciation of their lives. This was extremely uncomfortable. This particular worker had a supportive supervision system and was surviving in the job, but it was clear that the job of a nurse in a hospital amongst other nurses is far more comfortable.

Discussions with any health professionals attempting to work sensitively raises the issues of how close or how open the professional/client relationship should and can be. These issues of appropriate boundaries have to be addressed in training, since they are extremely complex and there are no hard and fast rules — except perhaps that support should be sought by anyone involved in supporting or caring for someone else. Individuals have very different attitudes to the amount or interpersonal closeness they feel they can or should bear. This varies from day to day, and situation to situation. Guilt and anxiety around these issues is often severe, whether the professional offers or refuses support of 'a listening ear'. Lack of psychological support for the professionals who make themselves emotionally available to clients may lead to burn-out or to increasing insensitivity.

A particular problem arises from the past history of people with disabilities. Often babies or small children with disabilities have experienced some kind of disruption in their relationship with their parents. Their families are more likely than others to have broken up. The effect on parents of having a disabled child can be extremely traumatic. The child concerned may as a result have had disturbed relations with carers all his or her life. This may make it hard for the child to relate to people as adults even when given the chance.

In Barcelona, a project which helps mothers to interact with their children with cerebral palsy is tackling this problem at its roots. Mothers come with their small babies during the day for several weeks to a special unit where their interaction is observed and discussed with specialised professionals and also informally with the other mothers. The effect on both children and mothers is remarkable. Rejection is dramatically reduced as the mothers learn how to handle their babies' unexpected physical reactions. As far as I am aware, there is nothing of its kind in Britain.

People with disabilities of any age may have been treated with lack of respect; in this case they may be more likely to treat helpers with lack of respect. A helper has to decide whether to be treated like this, to demand better treatment, or to leave. Any of these choices is problematical.

There is a general problem about the role of assisting someone in a task where they would not normally need to be assisted. The aim of simply and solely behaving as the arms, legs or mouthpiece of the person needing assistance turns out to be difficult to implement directly. The opinions and the feelings of the helper need to be taken into account, but it is not easy for the helper to decide at what point these should take priority in deciding whether to undertake a task or not.

In a discussion group, a woman using a Bliss board indicated to the facilitator what she wanted to say. The facilitator did not want to say it to the group and instead said that she felt things like that should be said in private. The woman concerned insisted that she did want to say it to the group and the facilitator finally said it. It concerned on-going incest.

It is hard to be in a position of power without authority. The facilitator's opinions about what should be said in groups conflicted with her opinion that people with disabilities should have the right to say what they want like anyone else. She felt bad afterwards that the woman had had to insist on her right to be heard, but felt equally bad about her responsibility for the effect on the group of the revelation.

> Staff in a day centre had difficulty in deciding how to behave towards a couple who were causing considerable disruption by their ostentatious flirting. The man was middle-aged and married and the woman was very young; he was wheelchair bound and she was able to help him considerably in spite of her own disabilities. The staff were afraid of misusing their power to assert their power to assert their own morality. The feeling that it was not up to them to pass judgement was strong, but was it up to them to provide more private accommodation for couples in the day centre or to demand certain standards of behaviour in their classes? They were also hampered by their belief that a flirtation was also going on between two senior members of staff who were in a similar relationship.

The conflicts here were complex. Staff had internal conflicts: did they have a right to speak their own opinion or not? They had conflicts within the group; some felt extra-marital affairs could be encouraged; others felt they were to be discouraged. They had conflicts arising from the fact that they had some power and authority in the day centre, but they felt this was illegitimate; at the same time, they had not succeeded in setting up a Users' Committee which could have an opinion on such tricky issues. They had conflicts perhaps between their beliefs and their own behaviour, and conflicts connected with their beliefs about the senior staff members' (suspected, hypothetical or platonic) affair. The two day centre users concerned probably also had conflicting feelings and beliefs which were reflected in the staff group.

Disability in general creates conflicts for the person who has it. These may be externalised so that others fight or argue. The handling of such external conflicts may affect the resolution of the internal conflict.

> From this point of view, a new light is thrown on the enormous amount of work which apparently is needed in order to enable a community to accept locally some new form of living arrangements for people who previously were institutionalised. Anyone moving out of their known home to a more independent form of living is likely to feel ambivalent. Some of the work done in the community may have value in helping the potential residents to resolve their own conflicts, particularly where they

themselves are involved in meeting local people and either arguing their own case or being present while others argue it.

### Envy

Some of the conflicts between people with disabilities and others arise from envy or fear of it. By envy I mean specifically *feelings of wanting to spoil something just because it is perceived as desirable but unattainable.*[5] These feelings are ultimately destructive both of others' happiness and one's own.

> A young woman with a new disability was complaining about her husband, her son, her mother and her friends. A telephone counsellor was trying to understand, saying comforting things which normally helped people. Nothing appeared to help. Finally, she said, 'It sounds as if the problem is you just hate everyone for being happy and OK, and I think that includes me – you can't bear it if I say anything helpful because that will make you feel even worse!' The young woman laughed with relief.

Professionals need careful discussion with supervisors to distinguish between envious criticism, directed at work (or abilities or characteristics) perceived originally as good, and justified criticism which attacks work which is simply bad. The two may be mixed together. Fear of envy may lead staff to disable themselves.

> A group of staff decided never to write in front of people they worked with who were illiterate. It did not occur to them to ask the people concerned what they thought about this.

### Guilt

Professionals often say they feel guilty at not being disabled themselves. This guilt can be quite paralysing, since any work or activity may be experienced as showing off an unfair advantage over the person who has any disability. Since they cannot actually be held responsible for the other person's disability, some complex psychological mechanism is involved here. Possibly the guilt refers to an unconscious sense of triumph over the disabled person; perhaps to an unconscious fantasy that the other person has the disability *instead* of them. It is clearly related to 'survivor guilt' which may be quite devastating in its effects.

A professional working with a group of disabled people told me how he felt quite paralysed by the sense that he was not disabled and they were. We talked of the fact that he had lost his small son recently and that this loss might by some be considered worse than the loss of the use of one's legs. The discussion made him feel better, and freed him to use his abilities in the service of the group.

## 'You have not experienced it therefore you cannot understand'

This is a sentiment which often enters into relations between people with disabilities and people without. It is used to challenge the professional perspective. It confronts professionals with the fact that their understanding is not superior to that of the client. It has been extremely important that this point of view should be established.

However, one of the results of this view is also an undermining of the professional's beliefs in the capacities they do have. Professionals may use it to excuse either their own reluctance to be involved with clients, or the supply of inferior services.

The question of counselling is particularly affected by this. There is a very important role and function for self-help groups. Meeting others who have suffered as you have can be extremely helpful. Part of the importance of such groups is the way in which they offer an opportunity for people with disabilities themselves to help others. However, there is always a danger – amongst non-professionals and professionals alike – that some people will use their 'helping' role to make themselves feel better by making others feel worse, inferior, envious or admiring towards them. Selection by those seeking help can counteract this in ordinary encounters; in situations where the helper has some authority, the authorising agency has a responsibility to attempt to ensure that this does not take place. Careful selection and on-going support (including formal or informal training) of volunteers is vital here.

Understanding of anything, including a particular disability, is strongly affected by experience. But the implication that only people with disabilities can understand other people with disabilities is false idealisation; it assumes that there is nothing more to people than their disabilities, and furthermore, that all disabilities are the same.

Professionals may be particularly vulnerable to accusations of not being disabled themselves when they too are unconsciously assuming that the disability is all there is to a person, and are scared of their own triumph or sense of superiority over the person with a disability.

One counsellor said that she felt guilty at first about enjoying counselling people with a chronic illness. As she tried to verbalise the content of the guilt she realised that she was assuming that the people she was counselling could have no pleasure or satisfaction in their own lives, and that they would therefore feel nothing but envy of her enjoyment. She finally came to the realisation that any of her clients might have a better sex life than she did: with this she lost her sense of guilt.

One way in which professionals handle their discomfort with the contrast between themselves and their clients is to seek out the 'disabilities' in their own lives.

A teacher in a school for physically handicapped children said she and the other staff used to say 'everyone has a handicap'. Her own handicap was that her voice was not good enough for her to join the national choir which had been her ambition. This helped her to deal with children being self-pitying and saying 'it's all right for you!' She felt she was trying to 'normalise' the children's sense of grievance against the world in order that they did not grow up unbearably self-centred and unable to relate to each other.

Clearly this approach has to be used with discretion. The sense of 'me too', or 'everyone has that problem' can be quite infuriating if it is used to deny the differences between people, to minimise their loss and to refuse sympathy when it is wanted.

Sometimes there is a sense of competitiveness involved: not only 'how ill I am compared with you' but also 'how badly the medical professions have behaved towards us' may be the subject of lively comparison in self-help discussion groups. This is most likely to arise when there is little sense that understanding and sympathy can be shared: where life is seen in terms of 'either you or me' rather than 'you and me'. Professionals may contribute towards establishing the existence of the one atmosphere or the other.

Where professionals can recognise and tolerate their own real disabilities and handicaps; their own fears of being mad; the ways they limit their own lives; their own dependence upon others, they can become more tolerant of others' disabilities and fears about them. Where they have recognised their own anxieties about being inferior or superior, victims or bullies, they may be more able to function in a way which does not require that their clients conform to one or other of these categories. This requires a level of self-awareness which may or may not be attainable within training courses.

Where the only required qualifications for a position are having a particular disability, the service may not be up to the highest standards. In some cases there seems to be a feeling that it is all right for people with disabilities to have an inferior service. There is a real difficulty here in bringing together valuable lessons learnt over the years by professionals of any kind, and the need to train and employ people who have disabilities themselves and have therefore been prevented from obtaining certain qualifications. The arguments are similar to those handled by the women's movement and race consciousness groups over the past twenty years. It seems that there are situations in which the requirement of having a particular disability may override all others; there are other situations where this is not the case.

> Action for Research into Multiple Sclerosis (ARMS) has confronted this problem. It provides a telephone counselling service for people with MS run entirely by counsellors who have MS themselves or live with someone who has it. They are carefully selected and trained for their ability to offer real support and to listen without imposing their own opinions. It also encourages people to use professional counsellors. These counsellors may or may not have MS: their qualifications are that they are good counsellors with some knowledge of MS, learnt partly from ARMS and partly from their work with clients who have it.

## Training implications

Training in the past specifically for working with people with disabilities has been extremely patchy. This means that many staff at present working in this field have had scarcely any training. Training has to address both this group and new recruits.

Innovative professionals need to present and discuss their work with other professionals. Specialist seminars, for example at the Tavistock Clinic in London, contribute to the development of new ideas and concepts. Publication of innovative work can help to raise awareness and to stimulate further initiatives which address the issues involved. Good supervision is also essential for all staff, however well trained, to provide the opportunity to examine and reflect upon work in progress.

Until it is normal for severely disabled people to make up a visible, positively interactional part of the general social world we live in, training has to provide corrective experiences for new recruits. It is necessary but not sufficient that workers should have experience with disabled clients; they also need experience with competent disabled colleagues.

Periods working with organisations such as the Derbyshire Centre for Integrated Living (DCIL), of the North Derbyshire Mental Health Services Project[6] where normalisation is put into practice, would obviously benefit trainees: the cost to the organisation has to be counted.

### 'Getting to know you' approach

Professionals in training for work with people with disabilities should be set the task of attempting to get to know the life situation, experiences and emotions of someone with disabilities. This person could be a potential client or a colleague. They would have to be prepared to be with the trainee for, say, an hour a week for the duration of the course, or cover a shorter period more intensively, and to communicate something of their life experience to the trainee. Group discussions for the trainees would allow the assumptions, observations, feelings and denials of the trainees to be examined and shared. Group discussions for the people with a disability offering their time in this way would allow them to share their experiences and could provide feedback for improving the training course.

> Where staff in a day centre were set the task of asking someone who had it what their multiple sclerosis meant to them, of a group of eight, only two did it. These two were astonished to find out what full past lives the people concerned had, and spoke of them with increased respect. This experience may imply that in spite of its value, many factors combine to make it hard to find time and enthusiasm actually to seek information from clients with a disability, which may explain partly why such a training method as that outlined above does not seem to be common.

### Staff of training courses

Training courses should have on the staff some people with obvious deformities or disabilities themselves. This is a principle used effectively by the Greater London Association for Disabled People (GLAD), DCIL and other disability organisations around the country. Both GLAD and DCIL use effective combinations of people with and without disabilities. These organisations are in a good position to train professionals.

It is clearly important when setting up courses that the staff running them should not either deny or idealise their own or others' disabilities and their implications. Ideally the same – high – criteria of professionalism and self-awareness would be demanded of the staff with disabilities as those without. However, we are at present in a situation where all these attitudes and skills are being newly learnt, and the training course may be training the trainers. Relations between the training staff may be at times very difficult, and it may be important to build in time for these relationship problems to be explored. The discoveries made during such exploration can then be used in the training of others.

Conflicts between people with disabilities and people apparently without can be brought into the open and dealt with constructively in a well-run course. Fear, hostility, denial, pity, frustration, irritation, disgust, protectiveness, distraction, curiosity, apprehension, demands for special treatment and a rejection of such special treatment, all of which can be aroused by disabilities, may also be examined and challenged in such a safe situation. This may well be preferable to leaving the professionals to learn entirely from their clients.

### Increase in closeness

It seems that where professionals can be helped to discuss with a client the effect the disability has on their interaction with other people, including the professional themselves, both client and professional may discover new potential and new pleasure in their interaction.

However, any increase in the sense of real understanding and closeness may raise anxieties unless the boundaries around the relationship are clear and firm. The differences and similarities between relations with paid staff and friendships need to be clarified. The professional may feel afraid of (or very guilty about) arousing desires for sexual or social closeness which they do not want to satisfy. This may hinder even minimal contact. The individual and professional stance on the question of assisting in other people's sexual relationships may also need to be clarified. This kind of difficulty also points to the need for continuing support for staff in handling questions which arise on a day to day basis.

### The role of self-help groups

There seems to be an important role for self-help organisations in educating the public in general and professionals in particular. Those with the greatest interest in improving the treatment of people with disabilities, be they mental or physical, are the people who have them, their families and friends. Where groups of such people get together and work towards changing attitudes, as has happened at ARMS for multiple sclerosis, in the Parkinson's Disease Society, in the National Schizophrenia Fellowship and in Age Concern, to mention but a few, new and effective publications and initiatives have emerged. The different views represented by the different organisations may help to clarify conflicts, not only between people with particular conditions and the medical profession but also between people with disabilities and their families.

Faced with hostility from the medical professions, some self-help groups have begun to employ their own professionals not only to provide them with the knowledge base they require, but also to challenge and change the medical professions from within. They threaten doctors' self-idealisation, by listening to patients, publishing what they say and offering access to information which doctors previously withheld.

Where people have traditionally been infantilised, such as those with Downe's syndrome, senility or other intellectual handicaps, there may be conflicts over suitable lifestyles and acceptable risks.[7] Socialisation (sometimes including covert or open rejection or actual abuse from parents or other carers) may have compounded handicaps and permitted or encouraged unnecessarily infantile or institutionalised behaviour, which has been taken as a reason for maintaining the 'child' status. Some family members may oppose more radical professional opinion, and call on their own professionals to vindicate past behaviour and maintain the status quo.

## Working with people suffering from psychotic states of mind

I want now to look at some of the special issues which arise for staff working with people who suffer from particularly disturbing states of mind.

### Sanity issues

Recent thinking about mental illness emphasises the sanity and 'normality' which coexists along with madness and psychosis in everyone. (By psychotic I mean 'out of touch with reality, external or internal'.) W. Bion is extremely illuminating about such interactions.

Staff trying to improve methods of working with people who are at times openly mentally disturbed have the difficult task of fostering the more sane states of mind, while trying to understand the more disturbed and disturbing. They are seldom helped in this task.

In an old-fashioned mental hospital, the divisions between patients and staff helped staff to maintain an exaggerated belief in the differences between them. An approach which emphasises some kind of equality between patients and staff (for example in organisations such as the Richmond Fellowship, deriving from the therapeutic community movement) removes this protection from staff. Staff therefore need help to handle fears of their own madness in a different way. Distancing themselves from their own madness by seeing it in patients is no longer acceptable. Training has generally failed to take full account of this except in the case of psychotherapy and psychoanalytical training, which requires that practitioners undergo long periods in the patient role, discovering their own insanity before being allowed to work with others.

Psychiatric staff are required to work with people suffering from some of the most destructive and self-destructive states of mind.

Pink Floyd's 'The Wall'[8] describes Roger Waters' view of a mental breakdown. The words include: 'Oh Babe; . . . Don't leave me now; . . . Remember the flowers I sent; . . . I need you; To put through the shredder in front of our friends; . . . How could you go when you know how I need you; to beat to a pulp on a Saturday night; . . . Don't leave me now; How can you treat me this way? . . . I don't need no arms around me . . .'

The fact that these states may be temporary, may coexist with more loving and creative states of mind, and are by no means exclusive to mental patients, does not prevent their being extremely disturbing. Desperate unhappiness and longing may be encountered along with cruelty, perversity, blame and rejection. Happiness, affection, caring and sanity in those around may be attacked as cruel teasing, or as hypocritical rather than genuine. It is often difficult to decide if such attacks are justified or not.

A 'normal' example of this would be a teenager interpreting parental concern as unreasonable prying into their affairs. The parents too may find it difficult to decide which it is. A more difficult situation would be a man who insists that his 7-year-old daughter liked having intercourse with him and that it was good for her. The defining of something extremely damaging as good is perverse; it may confuse the professionals as well as the child.

It is extremely difficult to deal with the effects and consequences of destructive or self-destructive states of mind without losing sight of both sanity and more caring feelings, either in the self or in others. A good body of knowledge is needed to clarify and make bearable the experiences of living or working with people who are very disturbed. Unfortunately, this knowledge is in its infancy. A thoroughly supportive managerial environment is also essential. Without these two sources of support, professionals themselves may become prey to cruelty, perversity, destructiveness and burn-out, just as were staff in the mental hospitals. Alternatively, as Menzies Lyth describes, the more mature staff simply leave.[9]

### Denial of madness

> A young graduate working in a residential hostel before training as a social worker was discussing a woman who lived there. This woman believed that rays were coming out of the television into her brain; the graduate said this was true; rays do come out of televisions. The woman said that a tennis player at Wimbledon was trying to kill her. The graduate did not want to admit that this was a delusion, but insisted that it could be true. He found it very difficult to believe that the people he worked with sometimes really saw things quite differently from him.

This graduate had very good intentions: he was trying to resist a 'them and us' division, and 'labelling'. He wanted to get to know the people he lived with. Unfortunately, he was confused – as the woman too was at times – about the distinctions between reality and madness. He did not help her to hold on to her sanity by ignoring the madness of her delusions.

The attempt to interpret insane behaviour as sane, to react in ways which are appropriate when the ground rules are those of sanity but are not appropriate at times when these rules no longer hold, can drive staff to breakdown or cynicism. We need to develop the ability to see people as they really are, including their crazy ideas, if we are to really understand them and ourselves.

### Training implications: mental disturbances

#### Lack of theoretical base
All the psychiatric conditions, including attempted suicide, alcoholism, delusions, paranoia, severe depression and obsessions may evoke quite negative reactions in staff. There is at present a lack

of training which includes sympathetic understanding of the experience of such states, and the effects they can have on the individual and on those around them. Teaching about such conditions has often been confined to description of symptoms rather than an assessment of the impact of such symptoms on a life.

Research by Kleinian psychoanalysts such as Bion and Rosenfeld into psychotic states of mind is beginning to have some kind of influence on professional work in this field, but as yet this is very limited. Psychoanalysis is unusual in mental 'treatments' in that it involves working in partnership with the analysand to understand in detail the whole personality rather than symptoms. It can only take place with the active participation and consent of the person concerned and is not confined to the disabled or ill. The insights gained are therefore quite unlike those of pharmacological or behavioural psychiatry. Attempts simply to understand and share emotional experiences are recognised as powerfully effective as well as extremely difficult. Some of the terrifying states of mind which lead to the psychoses have been sympathetically understood by such analysts.[10] This work has also enhanced perception of psychotic mechanisms in 'normal' people. Without a good theoretical base staff may not either observe or make sense of the behaviour and feelings of others or themselves in the presence of severe mental disturbances. They may be forced back on oversimplified behavioural or 'common sense' concepts which embody rejection of a particularly harsh kind, in direct reflection of the mental processes involved. In this situation staff may lose their sense of themselves or others as (ever) good, sane, caring people.

*Who needs training?*
With the closing down of mental hospitals, more mental health work will take place in community mental health centres, day centres and other non-hospital residential settings. Much work may be thrown on to the proprietors of private rooms to let, who are unlikely to be offered any training at all. Some will continue to take place in ordinary hospitals. People in any of these settings need to learn more about psychotic states of mind and how to live with them if they are not to repeat the mistakes of those working in the system they are to replace. Not only must they learn to demonstrate a new respect for the users of their centres, and new skills of management and perhaps advocacy, but they also have to learn how to handle their own reactions to other people's disturbed and disturbing behaviour.

Staff of community mental health centres also need to be trained and given the time to seek out and develop new ways of utilising and supporting local resources and of giving power to users themselves. Work with neighbours of people who have been moved out of mental hospitals of any kind may be important if they are not to overreact to odd behaviour through a sense of being unsupported.

Staff in the specialist units may perhaps have some hope of receiving such specialist training, though the present situation does not encourage optimism here. There is, for example, as yet no requirement that staff in drug abuse units should have their own psychotherapy to help them counter their own reactions to the self-destructiveness involved. Even the need for close supervision of such work is not always implemented at present.

As far as the general hospital is concerned, we already have evidence of the ways non-specialist nursing staff react to people in self-destructive states of mind. Attempted suicide is dealt with in general hospitals. The behaviour of both doctors and nurses towards people who try to kill themselves is often highly unsatisfactory.

> A girl who had taken an overdose was having her stomach pumped out. A nurse told her to make sure she succeeded next time.

Such reactions (and worse) on the part of the nursing staff are understandable, but they do not augur well for the future if more disturbed people are to be treated in general hospitals without the benefit of more and better training.

### Who should provide training?
The new psychiatric wards in general hospitals have the potential to influence the level of knowledge about psychotic states of mind within the whole hospital. Their staff could – if they had the resources and will – institute training programmes.

Ex-patients as well as their organisations have a role to play in conveying greater understanding of mental problems. Unfortunately, the provision for staff and staff training in hospitals is so limited that any training programme would be unlikely to receive sufficient priority to be implemented.

The new community mental health centres in theory could provide all kinds of educational programmes for professionals as well as for the general population. The Willesden Centre for Psychological Treatment is one initiative which offers both various outpatient treatment programmes for people with mental problems and training programmes for diverse local health workers. This work has uncovered a great local need which is as yet unsatisfied for more training and resources in the mental health field. If their funding is insufficient to support both, they may have to make difficult choices between input to the general population and input to professionals.

*Role of self-help organisations*
In the mental health field, the self-help organisations have already contributed enormously to general understanding and sympathy for the situation of the mentally disturbed and their families by publications, courses and publicity (see Chapter 5). More needs to be done, particularly in terms of educating the professionals.

## Summary

### Training implications of normalisation work

Staff attempting to change their ways of working in order to treat clients or patients more like people rather than 'the disabled' face difficulties, a number of which have been considered here.

Hostility and denial towards aspects of the disability and of the person who has it arise with all conditions. Other issues gain a different emphasis, depending on the client group and the staff group involved.

With mental handicap, some professionals are discovering that people with limited intellectual abilities may have emotional strengths and weaknesses which are not very different from people with university degrees.

In the field of physical handicap, respect for the brain may be easier to establish, and the difficulties be more focused on conflicts between people with disabilities and people apparently without. These external conflicts may reflect internal conflicts (in everybody) between parts of the self seen as 'disabled' and parts seen as 'not disabled'.

Staff working with people liable to psychotic states of mind (which alternate with and shade into non-psychotic states) have a different set of anxieties to handle. For them the issues around sanity are important: they are forced to raise questions not only about their client's sanity but also about their own, society's, and those above them in the organisational hierarchy.

It is clear that the issues raised by the desire to improve all aspects of life for people with any kind of disability require long and patient work on the part of professionals. There are no easy answers to the difficulties. If we do not discover and change some of our basic assumptions about disabilities, we run the risk of simply replacing one set of undesirable attitudes and behaviour with another.

The changes demanded of professionals include the need to recognise and accept both their own similarities with and differences from their clients. Work satisfaction needs to depend on clients running their own lives and making their own mistakes. Professionals have to give up attempts to impose control and begin to work in partnership, while maintaining certain boundaries. All this raises anxieties at the same time as opening up possibilities for a new kind of creative work and social life for both professional and client group.

## References

1. Wolfensberger, W., 'Social Role Valorisation: A Proposed New Term for the Principle of Normalisation', *Mental Retardation*, vol.21, no.6, 1983, pp. 234–9.
2. Menzies Lyth, I., *Containing Anxieties in Institutions* (London: Free Association Books, 1988).
3. Sinason, V., 'Smiling, Swallowing, Sickening and Stupefying: The Effect of Sexual Abuse on the Child'. *Psychoanalytic Psychotherapy*, vol.3, no.2, 1988, pp. 97–111.
4. Menzies Lyth, I., see 2 above.
5. Salzberger-Wittenburg, I., *Psychoanalytic Insight and Relationships* (London: Routledge & Kegan Paul, 1975).
6. Milroy, A. and Hennelly, R. 'Changing our Professional Ways', in Brackx, A. and Grimshaw, C., *Mental Health Care in Crisis* (London: Pluto Press, 1989).
7. Norman, A., *Rights and Risks* (London: Centre for Policy on Ageing, 1980).
8. 'The Wall', Pink Floyd. EMI records.
9. Menzies Lyth, I., see 2 above.
10. Spillius, E., *Melanie Klein Today*, 2 vols (London: Routledge & Kegan Paul, 1988).

'When I walk into the busy staffroom at college or join a room full of friends and see the switch, as if by reflex, to speaking and signing so that I can understand, I feel a glow of joy. This is how it should be because I am important and lovable enough to be included and when I am included, I am no longer disabled.'

'Maggie', in J. Campling, (ed.) *Images of Ourselves: Women with Disabilities*

# 5
# Creative Programming
*Richard Warner*

After nearly four decades of experience in treating psychosis with antipsychotic drugs and other psychoactive medication, it has become apparent that, despite optimal pharmacological treatment, many people who suffer from mental illness are left with substantial social and psychological deficits. Of those treated in the community, many suffer daily from psychotic symptoms, have few friends or social skills, are unable to work or properly take care of their basic needs and have no meaningful daily activity. They are bored and alienated – not true members of the communities in which they live, lacking a sense of self-worth or self-mastery. For some, relief from boredom and powerlessness is found in the use of street drugs which often tend to worsen their psychiatric symptoms. What more could be done to improve the outlook for people with mental illness? Can we build programmes which will help integrate them into society? Are there forms of social intervention which would allow these people to contribute more to their communities, to gain a feeling of purpose and belonging and to minimise the effects of their disorder?

In times and places other than the present-day industrial West, schizophrenia and other major mental disorders have proven to be relatively benign. Some of the early nineteenth-century establishments which made effective use of moral treatment, for example, appear to have often achieved good outcome from psychosis. The basic principles of this treatment approach, wherever they were properly applied, were the avoidance (as far as possible) of coercion, confinement and restraint and the development, instead, of individual self-control. Treatment settings were small and homelike and patients were encouraged to participate in work and social activities in an effort to create a normalising environment which would promote self-control and the maintenance of social skills and help integrate the person back into his or her home and community as early as possible.[1]

Although the benefits of moral treatment were not generally made available to the indigent in Britain,[2] in the American states, it appears,

114

they were more widely adopted and led to superior care in the public asylums.

In the heyday of early nineteenth-century industralising America, European travellers were struck by the quality of American asylums and the high recovery rates which they achieved through the application of the humane and normalising principles of moral treatment. Charles Dickens was favourably impressed by public and private hospitals in the New World in 1842,[3] and Captain Basil Hall, another English traveller, pointed out, in 1827, that the recovery rate of patients recently admitted to a prominent Connecticut hospital was substantially greater than that of recent admissions to similar British asylums.[4] Claims of high recovery rates – around 80 to 90 per cent of acute patients – in US asylums of the period were common:[5] and although later psychiatrists attempted to denigrate these claims as the 'cult of curability',[6] available figures[7] and follow-up data[8] appear to confirm that these results were outstandingly better than those of British hospitals of the time or the achievements of hospitals on either side of the Atlantic in the latter decades of the century.

Similarly striking are the many studies which indicate that in the Third World today schizophrenia appears to follow a less malignant course than in the West.[9–12] Two different, multicentre WHO projects, using standardised diagnostic and outcome measures, have now demonstrated that people suffering from schizophrenia in Third World villages are much more likely than Western patients to recover from a psychotic episode and return to an adequate level of social functioning.[13,14] If there is a common explanation for the good outcome from psychosis in young, industrialising America and in rural parts of the Third World today, it may be that in both settings labour conditions were or are favourable for the rehabilitation and social integration of marginally functional people. In early America, an extreme labour shortage encouraged the employment of the disabled,[15] and in Third World villages the subsistence economy allows the employment of many who would be excluded from a wage-labour force burdened with significant levels of unemployment.[16]

Can we establish clinical programmes, in the current welfare climate, which will capture some of the normalising principles of moral treatment; and, in these times of high unemployment, are there ways to make work and other types of productive activity available to people with mental illness which will help them combat the corrosive effects of alienation?

## Clinical programmes

Psychiatric treatment, by labelling people as abnormal, removing them, at times, to institutions, and using coercion to control and treat them, is inherently anti-normalising, though its clinical effects may work in the reverse direction and help the person's process of recovery and reintegration. Clinical programmes can be so designed, however, that the anti-normalising tendency is minimised. This can be especially true if we create alternatives to the psychiatric hospital – the most coercive, confining and socially disintegrative component of the treatment system.

### A community-based, acute-treatment facility

Cedar House is a large house on a busy residential street in Boulder, Colorado. Staffed, as one would staff an acute psychiatric hospital ward, with nurses, a psychiatrist and mental health workers, it functions as an alternative to psychiatric hospital for the acutely disturbed patients of the Mental Health Center of Boulder County. Like a hospital, it offers all the usual diagnostic and treatment services (except for electroconvulsive therapy). Routine medical evaluations are performed on the premises: patients requiring advanced medical and neurological investigation are referred to local physicians and outpatient hospital departments. Unlike a hospital, it is homelike, unlocked and non-coercive. At $110 a day, it costs less than a quarter as much as private psychiatric hospital treatment, where daily charges routinely exceed $500 a day.

As far as possible, Cedar House has the appearance of a middle-class home, not a hospital. The house is carpeted and furnished with pictures and shelves of books, a cat shares the comfortable furniture with residents, and, on winter nights, a fire burns in the hearth. Staff and patients interact casually, eat together and share household duties; but, because of the short length of patient stay and the necessity for managers to exercise close control over admissions and discharges (in order to make room for new acute admissions at all times), a full-scale therapeutic community with patient government is not considered feasible.

Residents and visitors come and go fairly freely through the unlocked doors. Staff must encourage patients to comply willingly with treatment and house rules: no one can be strapped down, locked in or medicated by force. Many patients are treated involuntarily at Cedar House under the provisions of the state mental illness statute;

they accept necessary restrictions because the alternative is hospital treatment, which virtually none prefers. The people who cannot be treated in the house are those who are violent, threatening or repeatedly walk or run away. In practice, most people with schizophrenia or psychotic depression can be treated in the facility through all phases of their illness, and many with mania can also be managed successfully. It is clear, however, that the hospital has not been entirely replaced by this open-door setting: a small number of highly disturbed people must still be treated, at least initially, in a closed hospital ward.

There is no doubt that many of the people treated at Cedar House would be subject to more coercive measures, such as mechanical restraints and seclusion, if they were admitted to a psychiatric hospital. These control measures are very freely used in US psychiatric wards. On the acute admission unit of one California hospital, for example, 44 per cent of patients were locked in seclusion for varying periods of time.[17] Avoiding the seclusion room experience must be seen as a significant benefit, for it colours and dominates the person's view of his or her illness. When a group of hospital patients were asked to illustrate themselves and their illness, over a third spontaneously drew pictures of the seclusion room. Even a year after the hospital stay, the experience of seclusion, with its associated feelings of fear and bitterness, symbolised for many the entire psychiatric illness.[18]

Substantially cheaper than hospital care, an acute residential treatment facility such as Cedar House is a money-saver for an agency which would otherwise be contracting with private hospitals for acute treatment for patients. A psychiatric service which is not responsible for the costs of hospital care or which already incorporates an established hospital unit as part of its treatment system would have a more difficult time justifying the costs of such a programme. The fixed costs of such a facility would make it cost-inefficient, also, for a small agency serving a catchment area much below 200,000 persons. For an agency which can realise savings on hospital costs, however, an acute treatment unit like Cedar House allows treatment decisions to be made at a more measured pace than would be possible under the financial pressure of an expensive hospital stay, and it makes drug-free treatment of psychotic illness possible in selected cases. Treatment without antipsychotic drugs can be offered, for example, to those who are experiencing their first psychotic episode and to those who fail to show significant benefit from these medications.

### Therapeutic households

A completely non-institutional alternative to psychiatric hospital, much more normalising but distinctly more expensive than Cedar House, has been established by another agency in Boulder. Maitri Psychological Services, a programme affiliated with the East − West psychology department of a Buddhist university, the Naropa Institute, has developed a system of 'therapeutic households' for the treatment of people with psychotic disorders. In this programme, one psychotic patient is treated in his or her own home by a team of therapists, some of whom live in the same household with the patient. The therapists try to establish a healthy, family-style environment for the patient, helping him or her to learn basic living and interactional skills, develop recreational and vocational interests and expand the horizons of his or her life. Therapists spend time with the patient in a variety of settings and activities − hiking mountain trails, playing basketball and chess, cleaning house and discussing politics, religion and philosophy. The goals of therapy vary from patient to patient but might include the person becoming more composed and focused on the present moment, developing self-confidence and self-discipline and learning connections between his or her actions and their consequences.[19] Minimal doses of medication are used.

This intensive, normalising and integrating treatment approach incorporates the key ingredients of moral treatment which seemed to produce good outcome from psychosis in the early years of the last century (see references 4 − 8). Like moral management, the Maitri approach appears to be effective in changing the course of the illness. One highly disturbed, self-destructive, young man with a long-standing psychosis, for example, who, even in a model community treatment programme, experienced many painful relapses and hospital admissions each year, showed a considerable improvement in his quality of life and a dramatic decrease in hospital use when he was treated by the Maitri team.[20] This is perhaps the treatment one would choose for one's own close relative if he or she became psychotic. Like moral management, however, this form of treatment is expensive (around $200 − 300 a day) and few people can afford it. More to the point, no health insurance plans will pay for it. The programme in fact has been temporarily suspended, in part, due to shortage of sufficiently well-heeled customers.

## A household for the hospital-bound

In a cooperative venture, however, the Naropa Institute and the Mental Health Center of Boulder County have developed a new, cost-effective hospital alternative which uses the Maitri approach. Friendship House is a long-term, intensive-treatment household for five, very disturbed, young or middle-aged adults. Each of these patients (two men and three women) has been ill for over a decade with a brittle psychosis which has shown relatively little benefit from psychiatric medication. Each is somewhat uncooperative with treatment and is so volatile and lacking in social skills that he or she has been unable to live outside an in-patient setting for more than a few weeks or months since the illness began, even when he or she has been surrounded with an elaborate array of community supports. These people represent a new generation of the severely ill who have become chronically institutionalised in an era when few indigent people in the US stay in a hospital for any time at all.

Within the household, each resident has his or her own team, comprised of a part-time therapist (paid) and four part-time psychology interns and volunteers (all unpaid). Each member of this team also works with a second resident, so that five interlocking teams (totalling twenty people) are responsible for the treatment of the five patients. The remaining staff include two resident house-parents and a part-time programme director. All these staff work with the residents to create a therapeutic community and learning environment in which respect, compassion and openness are core values. The achievements of the programme during its first year have been: (a) four of the five patients are still living in the house and doing well (the fifth had to return to in-patient care and was replaced by a new resident), and (b) all four of the original residents have graduated to voluntary status after years of involuntary treatment under the state mental illness statute. None of them wants to leave.[21]

Another achievement of the programme is that the entire cost ($86 a day per patient) has been covered by a delicate combination of Medicaid health insurance, county foster-care funds and the resident's social security income. Meanwhile, five expensive in-patient beds (four at Cedar House and one at the state hospital) have been vacated by the patients who have moved into Friendship House, and these beds have become available to meet the pressing need for the treatment of other acutely ill patients.

Unfortunately, the complexities of the US health insurance system are such that only about half of the patients who might move out of hospital and benefit from a setting like Friendship House qualify for funding. Much of the ingenuity which goes into developing a model treatment programme in the USA is expended, not on the therapeutic design (that part is relatively easy), but on finding ways to fund the project through a health care and social service system whose elaborate network of rules has been established with the principal aim of preventing the funding programme's costs expanding, but which ultimately prevents the creation of cost-effective solutions. It is to be hoped that current experiments in capitation schemes for people with serious mental illness, which are taking place in different parts of the country, will eventually lead to comprehensive funding programmes in which 'the dollar follows the patient' into whichever programme best meets his or her needs.

### Intensive community treatment

Without an adequate system of out-patient care, the best hospital alternatives will find themselves overwhelmed by 'revolving-door patients'. The patients will simply revolve in through the doors of the new, domestic-style facility instead of the doors of the old institution. To combat this problem, some mental health centres in the United States have developed intensive community treatment and case management programmes, many of them modelled after the programme developed by Stein and Test in Madison, Wisconsin.[22] The Madison model aims to improve the quality of life for mentally ill people in the community and to prevent unnecessary hospital admissions by surrounding them with a comprehensive array of services. Programme staff assume responsibility for helping each client acquire basic material resources, such as food, clothing and housing; teaching the person basic skills, such as cooking and budgeting; helping solve real-life problems: interceding for the client with community agencies and agents, such as landlords; and making assertive efforts to keep the person in treatment. The Madison programme may be thought of as a day treatment programme turned upside down. Instead of the person coming into a day care facility and fitting into the institutional framework, the Madison staff are mobile – they go out to the client, help him or her to shop or find an apartment, accompany the person to appointments and develop an individualised treatment plan which will serve his or her needs best.

The staff of the Mental Health Center of Boulder County have built a similar, intensive community care programme for the 20 per cent of the centre's psychotic clients who are at greatest risk of relapse. These people tend to be those who have difficulty meeting their basic needs. They may have continuous psychotic symptoms, poor judgement, or substance-abuse problems: they may be quite non-compliant with treatment or too disorganised to keep appointments reliably. (The remaining 80 per cent of the centre's psychotic clients, who are less severely disabled, are seen once a week, or less often, in standard, office-based, out-patient treatment, which proves to be sufficient to prevent relapse.) The mobile community support team operates out of a large, old, fraternity house near the university campus. Many of the team's clients live in supervised or unsupervised, rent-subsidised housing which is owned or managed by the Mental Health Center. Caseloads are small; each therapist is responsible for about fifteen people. (A reasonable caseload on a standard out-patient team would be about thirty-five clients for each therapist.) Therapists' schedules on the community treatment team are flexible and patients can be seen as often as necessary – about half see a therapist daily. During the first few years of the team's operation, the number of days the clients spent in hospital were halved. The savings in hospital costs has offset all the additional expense of operating the intensive case management team.

In many ways, the services provided by the community treatment team could be described as controlling or paternalistic. A few of the clients are involuntarily enrolled in treatment under the provisions of the mental illness statute. About half of the clients attend daily to take their medication under supervision, to ensure compliance, and about half have their money (from their monthly social security cheque) managed by a therapist and distributed as a small daily or weekly allowance. The alternative for most of these people, however, would be some combination of the following – homelessness, hunger, victimisation, jail, symptom exacerbation, self-inflicted harm, repeated brief hospital admissions or long hospital stays. To live on the street or in a shelter, to eat out of dustbins and to sojourn repeatedly in gaol and hospital is not to be an integrated member of the society. It is for this reason that a programme of effective, if somewhat controlling, out-patient treatment is included in a chapter on approaches to normalisation.

## Vocational programmes

Work is a normalising and integrating force which is fundamental to the maintenance of a sense of self-worth and self-mastery. It is the primary way in which people around the world define their social roles and develop their sense of belonging and contribution to society. While much routine work in modern industrial society has an alienating quality, many would consider long-term unemployment to be the most alienating condition (see reference 16). We could certainly do worse than to concentrate our efforts at social integration of people with mental illness on vocational rehabilitation. In practice, however, such programmes are often not as effective as we might hope.

Marginally functional, mentally ill workers find it extremely hard to obtain and hold jobs in an industrial society in which 'full' employment is defined as being around 4 to 6 per cent unemployment.[23] The jobs which such workers can obtain tend to be unskilled entry level or temporary positions which are unrewarding and, except during times of high unemployment, unattractive to other workers. Sheltered workshops, though they offer opportunities for training and occupation, cannot be considered to be particularly normalising and, during hard times, may be unable to obtain work contracts and to provide employment for those in need. Workshops for people with disabilities in fact may get into cut-throat competition with one another when the economy turns sour, and those which cannot call upon a large subsidy to allow them to underbid other workshops or those which do not switch to using higher functioning, more productive workers are likely to be forced to close.

## Supported employment

A greater degree of social integration may be achieved through sheltered employment in industry. A number of agencies, such as Fountain House, in New York City, and Thresholds, in Chicago, have been successful with vocational approaches which have been termed transitional employment or continuous supported employment.[24] Under these programmes, agency staff find a variety of job slots in private industry, place mentally ill clients in the positions, train each client how to perform the job, closely monitor his or her work performance from day to day, and provide on-the-job support and counselling. In the transitional employment model, clients are supposed to graduate at the end of a specific period (three to nine months) and move on to another job in the competitive labour market: in a continuous supported employment programme, the client may hold the job and receive supervision and counselling for as long as he or she wishes. The latter model is clearly preferable for clients with continuous, fluctuating disability from mental illness. Even at Fountain House, where the transitional employment model has been used to greatest advantage, few clients graduate successfully – most circulate through a succession of transitional positions.

The close attention these programmes offer greatly increases the client's chances of success, as those who suffer from psychosis are likely to experience an exacerbation of symptoms under the stress of learning a new job and meeting new people. Immediate counselling can reduce stress and symptoms and decrease the likelihood that the patient will leave or be fired. Employers generally welcome the opportunity to cooperate with a programme of this type as they can expect it to keep their entry level slots filled and relieve them of the responsibility of repeatedly training new staff in, what would otherwise be, high-turnover positions. Clients, moreover, are attracted to any programme, such as Thresholds, which can promise a job to those who participate. Why are there not more such programmes?

Funding for vocational services in the USA is available through the federal Department of Vocational Rehabilitation but it has proved difficult to obtain money for supported employment projects. Departmental requirements for continued funding are based on a model of serving people with physical disabilities: the department expects a substantial proportion of the clients to be successfully trained, placed in work and discontinued from services within a specific period of time. The notion of continuous supported employment is foreign to this model.

### Client-run businesses

The prospects are no more optimistic for another exciting vocational and reintegrative approach – client-run businesses. Although such ventures offer theoretical advantages of greater normalisation of lifestyle, improved status and greater flexibility of work demands for disabled workers, they may not be viable under usual economic conditions. A large proportion of small businesses fail within a year or two of being established. Client-run businesses, operating with the additional disadvantage of employing marginally functional workers, are even less likely to succeed. The early Fairweather Lodge models, in which previously institutionalised patients lived together and worked in teams which contracted to provide janitorial and similar services to area businesses, were generally successful only as long as some form of financial subsidy was available. The first Fairweather Lodge, developed in a prosperous part of the San Francisco Bay area of California in 1963, nearly collapsed when research funds were withdrawn and only survived because residents' earnings were supplemented by Veterans Administration pensions.[25] Later replications of the model, often operating under harsher economic circumstances, have encountered trouble in finding work contracts and have generally required substantial subsidies to survive.[26]

One response to this problem is for the business to employ more high-functioning disabled workers. At Remploy (a British company employing disabled people at a large number of factories producing consumer goods) fewer than 5 per cent of the employees suffer from major mental illness; many factories employ no people with mental disability at all. Even so, the company requires substantial government subsidy to offset business losses. It would be cheaper in fact to put Remploy's disabled workers on social security than to keep them at work.[27]

Given these problems of low productivity and uncompetitiveness, mental health service administrators are unlikely to run the risks of underwriting a client-run business. An attempt to start a client-run janitorial service at the author's mental health centre, in Boulder, Colorado, for example, had to be abandoned after a few months. The work could not be done as well, for the same rate, as by competing local contractors.

An intriguing idea proposed by Denver-based community psychiatrist and entrepreneur, Paul Polak, which he has drawn from his own successful development projects for peasants and refugees in the Third World, suggests a direction which might prove more viable for client-run businesses. The business would *aim to provide a service or product to other people with psychiatric disability and to related groups in the community*. The first step in such a venture would be an analysis of the budget of a number of people with mental disability to determine their major expenses and sources of income. An analysis of income allows an evaluation of the costs, benefits and incentives associated with productive activity. Many people with a fluctuating level of psychiatric disability, for example, might not want to risk the loss of their social security income by obtaining regular, but less secure, paid employment. The major expenses are likely to be food and housing, with recreation, transportation, alcohol, street, drugs, cigarettes and medication being other significant cost items. This analysis should suggest ways in which a consumer-run business could supply an essential service or product, keep the profit circulating within the group and thus increase the group members' overall expendible income. Although this approach might reinforce the psychiatric 'ghetto', it offers a number of potential advantages. Having a targeted, 'captive', group of customers would increase the competitive advantage and financial viability of the business, and consumers might be productively employed without putting their social security income in jeopardy.

Successful examples of such ventures may be seen around the United States. In the San Francisco Bay area, a group of people who have suffered from mental illness operate a cooperative apartment complex. In Utah, a mental health service consumer organisation manages a housing programme with a half-a-million dollar annual budget. Consumer-run clubhouses in various cities provide cheap meals, recreation, education and other services for the members. A coffee shop in Vermont, run by mental health centre clients, serves a fairly broad clientele, including a large number of customers from the mental health centre. With the provision of modest amounts of venture capital (seed money), training and help with organisational development, such businesses may begin to flourish. They are just a part, however, of a broader social development which holds out the prospect of empowering people with mental illness, decreasing their alienation and improving their access to necessary services. With the growth of the mental health services consumer movement we are seeing the development of a new phenomenon in psychiatry — consumers as providers of service.

## Consumer-operated services

Why is empowerment so important? In a study of people in community treatment for a psychotic disorder at the Mental Health Center of Boulder County, we found that gaining a sense of mastery over one's life (an internal locus of control) appears to be central to attaining a high level of functioning and good outcome from the illness. Contrary to the usual assumption within the profession, we found that people do not routinely achieve a better outcome if they accept that they suffer from a mental disorder. Acceptance of illness has to be coupled with an internal locus of control in order for the patient to fare better. Unfortunately, the stigma attached to mental illness is such that acceptance of the label tends to be linked to low self-esteem and a poor sense of self-mastery: patients who accept that they are ill and have an internal locus of control are rare.[28]

Our research suggests that we need to focus our efforts as much on helping clients develop a sense of mastery as we do on persuading them that they are ill. The opportunities, however, for teaching people how to develop self-control and self-mastery within the inevitably controlling psychiatric system are strictly limited. Independent consumer organisations, which allow people to escape the paternalism of psychiatry and to develop roles in which they display competence and self-sufficiency while offering something of value to others, may open new routes to recovery.

## Consumer organisations

Consumer-run service-delivery programmes are becoming increasingly common in the United States, matching the growing influence of the mental health consumer movement nationwide. Two national organisations, the National Mental Health Consumer Association and the National Alliance of Mental Patients vie for membership, sponsor national conferences, send speakers to professional meetings, combat stigma through media presentations and lobby for political objectives. Consumers are appointed to the governing boards of many local mental health centres, and state regulations in California require that the boards of residential facilities include consumer members.

Utah possesses a particularly well-developed statewide network of seventeen local mental health consumer organisations. Each group is a non-profit corporation providing mutual support and advocacy for people in psychiatric care. Some are autonomous civic groups while others are associated with a mental health centre. Many conduct fundraising activities, such as dances and car washes, while others operate consumer-run businesses — a cafe, for example. One of these local organisations has developed a drop-in centre and (as mentioned above) a cooperative housing project with a half-a-million dollar budget. Another group operates a supportive rap-line, and another has established a statewide speakers' bureau of consumers, family members and professionals. All these local groups are chapters of the statewide U-Can-Du organisation which has an office in the state Division of Mental Health. The statewide organisation is run by a board of directors comprised of seven consumers and two mental health professionals, all of whom are elected by the member groups. From the outset, mental health professionals have been involved in the growth of Utah's consumer network, and they continue to be viewed as partners and supporters. U-Can-Du employs a staff of three consumers; holds an annual state consumer conference and is involved in system advocacy, providing input in the state mental health planning process. The board of U-Can-Du manages a budget of $50,000 which is provided, almost entirely, by a federal grant from the National Institute of Mental Health.[29]

### Consumers as case managers

Some programmes which create service-provider roles for mental health consumers are not independent consumer ventures. A Colorado non-profit vocational organisation, the Regional Assessment and Training Center, with the support of the state Division of Mental Health, has created a novel and successful programme in which people who suffer from a major mental illness, but function at a high level, are trained to perform case management duties within the community mental health system. In the Denver Consumer Case Manager Project, trainees receive twenty-one credit-hours of college education during six weeks of classroom training and a fourteen-week field placement. Classroom courses include mathematics, writing, interviewing techniques, case management skills, crisis intervention and professional ethics. Following the supervised internship in a community mental health programme, trainees earn a certificate from the Community College of Denver and are placed in employment with a community programme serving people with severe mental disorder. As case manager aides, the programme graduates work under the supervision of a professional case manager, providing a number of services to their clients, including help with budgeting, applying for welfare entitlements, finding housing, and offering advice and support around treatment, work, interpersonal and other issues. Over 85 per cent of the programme graduates are currently successfully employed in case management jobs. In 1988–9, the third year of the programme's operation, between thirty and forty new consumer graduates were trained and placed in employment in the Colorado community mental health system.[30]

Until now, funding for case manager aide training and salaries has come from special project-development grants. One may reasonably ask, will the programme survive when mental health centres have to find the salaries for these consumer staff within their own, limited budgets? So far the signs are that these aides will be retained – for a number of reasons. They are cheaper than professional staff (salaries are around $10,000 per annum); they perform tasks which do not require advanced training and which the professionals are pleased to see others take on; and they achieve some things which professionals cannot. In particular, they serve as role models for clients who are struggling to manager their lives better and they can effectively reduce the antagonism and resistance which many clients show towards treatment. The consumer case managers also raise the staff and patient level of optimism about outcome from major mental illness. The goal of the project organisers is to transfer the responsibility for operation of the programme to a consumer group, in due course, and to convert it into a consumer-run business.

So successful has the programme been, that the Regional Assessment and Training Corporation is now developing training programmes to place clients in other positions in the mental health system, such as client advocates and drop-in centre managers. In Pueblo, Colorado, a programme has already been developed which employs mental health consumers as residential-care-facility staff.

### Peer counsellors for in-patients

In San Francisco, California, a social worker, who is also a mental health consumer, has developed another innovative programme in which consumers provide services to patients in a psychiatric setting. Carol Patterson trains and supervises people who have previously suffered episodes of mental illness to be peer counsellors for patients in a locked, acute treatment unit of San Francisco General Hospital. Following training, the peer counsellor is assigned to spend time at regular intervals with a patient newly admitted to the hospital unit in order to offer advice and support throughout the hospital stay. The peer counselling is quite distinct from the professional psychotherapy and psychiatric treatment which the patient receives: only in unusual circumstances does the peer counsellor talk to the staff about information gathered from the patient. Counselling by someone who has experienced in-patient psychiatric treatment helps humanise the treatment process, and the programme is viewed positively by staff and patients alike.[31]

### Consumer support groups

Similar kinds of support are being offered to out-patients with mental illness by consumer-run support groups. The Denver Social Support Group, established by Esso Leete, a woman who has suffered from schizophrenia since her teenage years, has met weekly for several years, helping people handle daily stresses, learn to manage their illnesses more effectively, fight the effects of stigma and stereotyping and increase their sense of personal power.[32] Across the nation, groups of this type are becoming increasingly popular. They often expand to become local chapters of statewide consumer organisations linked by newsletter, computer bulletins and annual conferences. Some state mental health authorities, such as Colorado, have perceived the advantages of consumer groups and networks of this type and have established small grant programmes to foster their growth.

### Clubhouses

Organisations such as Fountain House, in New York City, and Thresholds, in Chicago, have gained national and international prominence for establishing a model in which people with mental illness are involved in running a programme which meets many o their recreational, socialisation and vocational needs. Fountain House has been awarded a number of substantial grants to enable them to help agencies replicate their model in other communities around the country. These programmes, deservedly, have been highly praised for their achievements, but they have also been criticised for the limited extent to which consumers are involved in running the organisations. At Thresholds, for example, clients are called 'members' and they are routinely employed in a number of low-level positions in the day to day operation of the clubhouse (such as food service and reception duties) but they do not play a role in the management of the agency. Recently, however, a number of truly consumer-run clubhouses have sprung into being.

The Spiritmenders Community Center, in San Francisco, is such a project. Established by the San Francisco Network of Mental Health Clients, the programme is democratically run, funded and maintained solely by mental health service consumers. It offers a number of activities and services, including a safe place to drop in and socialise and education for its members and for the general public, and it aims to empower its members through peer counselling, advocacy and fostering self-advocacy. Members clearly do not see the centre as being part of the traditional mental health system. Richard Hasher, one of the organisers, reports that 'efforts are made to prevent those situations that force individuals to receive involuntary services and/ or other mental health services'.[33]

### Coopting consumers

Cooptation by the professional system of care is perceived to be a hazard by many consumer activists, especially where professional staff and consumers join forces to operate a programme. The basic danger is that consumers may be given token membership and not real power: on governing boards, planning committees or, at educational meetings, the consumer may be present but not heard. One consumer activist, speaking in a poorly attended symposium at the 1989 Annual Meeting of the American Psychiatric Association, illustrated the problem of being coopted by well-intentioned professionals in the following way. 'In the old days,' she commented, 'we used to be outside this building demonstrating and we would have crowds of psychiatrists watching us. Now we're inside, and there's nobody here.'

This issue produces tension, for example, at San Francisco's Tenderloin Self-Help Center – a drop-in programme which trains some of its own users to serve as volunteers and eventually as paid staff. The centre, which was established in response to an organised community effort by the residents of the inner city Tenderloin district, is open twenty-four hours a day, seven days a week, providing recreation and peer counselling for indigent and homeless mentally ill and substance-abusing people, many of whom refuse to attend standard psychiatric treatment facilities. The issues debated by staff and users of the programme include to what extent the centre should be user governed, community controlled or part of the formal mental health care system.[34]

Although cooptation is a danger, it is apparent that consumers are not sufficiently organised in many areas to create needed programmes without some outside help. In Boulder, Colorado, for example, many of the users of the mental health centre felt that a drop-in centre would help relieve the boredom and isolation of their lives: yet, there was no consumer group with enough cohesion to get such a programme started. In an attempt to get an independent drop-in centre started, mental health centre staff and managers met weekly with a small group of consumers to develop a consumer-run facility. The mental health centre provided space in one of its own buildings for the initial operation of the programme (although, clearly, an independent location, if available, would have been preferable), technical assistance with organisation and publicity, and consultation about sources of funding for training, staffing and space. The original plan, which called for the programme to be directed by a board of consumer volunteers and operated by trained consumer staff, has not proved successful. The necessary funding could not be found and the consumer organisation is not yet large and active enough to manage such a project. Instead, the centre staff and consumers have decided to establish a Fountain House style of clubhouse with more professional staff involvement, for which funding is more readily available.

The local Alliance for the Mentally Ill has proved to be a valuable source of support in developing programmes with more consumer involvement. This organisation of (primarily) relatives of people with mental illness has developed a strong national network and political lobby in the United States over the past decade. The direct consumer movement and the Alliance have some differences of philosophy. Whereas the Alliance movement has advocated strongly for a biomedical approach to mental illness and increased control over non-compliant patients, the direct consumer movement is more concerned about the social origins of mental disorder, and has a distaste for involuntary treatment. Some consumer groups, in fact, reject the concept of mental illness and are antagonistic towards all traditional psychiatric treatment (see Chapter 4). Despite these differences, there are signs that the Alliance and a segment of the direct consumer movement are beginning to join forces, with consequent changes in their philosophical positions. (The Colorado Alliance for the Mentally Ill, for example, now has direct consumers as members of its executive committee. These consumer members were influential in the committee's recent decision not to support the formal mental health system in fighting a court ruling which weakened the capacity of mental health agencies to treat patients involuntarily.) The result of this partnership may be that the older, better organised Alliance chapters will assist fledgling direct consumer groups to establish and operate support groups and drop-in centres. This can already be seen to be happening in some areas.

## Conclusion

For many years after the Second World War, the revolution in the care of people with mental illness in Northern Europe sought to reverse the damage caused by coercive, restrictive and regimenting total institutions. Hospital wards were decorated and furnished in a more domestic style, ward doors were unlocked, the sexes were allowed to mix, staff and patient power relationships shifted under the influence of the therapeutic community, and long-institutiona-lised patients were moved into the community. As a result of these revoluntionary changes, observers could see patients lose the symptoms of their institutional neurosis – the aimless pacing, mannerisms, mutism, passivity, incontinence and sudden aggression – which had long overlain their psychosis.

Now we are confronted with a new problem. The institutional neurosis has been replaced by an existential neurosis which is a product of the psychotic person's alienation in the community. Meaninglessness is one of the core existential concerns which confronts any individual,[35] and many people with mental illness face lives of profound purposelessness. Their days are empty of productive activity, their social relationships are few and often dependent and unrewarding.[36] According to Salvador Maddi,[37] among others,[35] existential neurosis, in its most severe form, presents as chronic aimlessness, meaninglessness and apathy coupled with boredom, depression and loss of a sense of personal value and mastery. Many people with long-standing mental disability display these features. In one recent study, when people in community treatment for psychosis were interviewed about their lives, their principal complaints were of boredom and (among the men) unemployment – both rated as much more problematic than psychotic symptoms.[38] Many professionals suspect that the high prevalence of drug and alcohol abuse among the mentally ill – half of one recent study sample,[39] is in part, a consequence of the empty, alienated lives which many psychotic people lead. As outlined in the opening paragraphs of this chapter, the outcome from schizophrenia appears to be much less severe in Third World and full-employment settings, where psychotic people are rehabilitated to a productive role in society and where the features of the illness are not magnified by alienation.

We now know how to reduce relapse in psychosis dramatically through intensive community treatment, though the political will to apply this solution widely is not yet manifest. If we are to combat alienation and the existential neurosis which continues to cripple people with mental illness who are sustained in the community, we must apply a new solution – engagement in purposeful activity (see reference 35). This is why, in the absence of opportunities for productive work, an adequate community mental health programme must harness consumer power in running its own organisations and programmes for self-help, and must transfer to the community lessons about patient government, empowerment, and staff and patient role-blurring learned in the hospital-based therapeutic communities of the 1950s and 1960s.[40]

## References

1. Jones, K., *A History of Mental Health Services* (London: Routledge & Kegan Paul, 1972).
2. Parry-Jones. W.L., *The Trade in Lunacy: A Study of Private Madhouses in England in the Eighteenth and Nineteenth Centuries* (London: Routledge & Kegan Paul, 1972).
3. Dickens, C., *American Notes for General Circulation* (Harmondsworth: Penguin, 1972).
4. Hall, B., *Travels in North America in the Years 1827 and 1828* (Edinburgh: Cadell, 1829).
5. Bromberg, W., *From Shaman to Psychotherapist: A History of the Treatment of Mental Illness* (Chicago: Henry Regnery, 1975).
6. Deutsch, A., *The Mentally Ill in America* (New York: Columbia University Press, 1949).
7. Thurnam, J., *Observations and Essays on the Statistics of Insanity* (London: Simpkin, Marshall, 1845; reprinted New York: Arno Press, 1976).
8. Bockoven, J.S., *Moral Treatment in Community Mental Health* (New York: Springer, 1972).
9. Murphy, H.B.M. and Raman, A.C., 'The Chronicity of Schizophrenia in Indigenous Tropical Peoples', *British Journal of Psychiatry*, vol.118, 1971, pp. 489–97.
10. Waxler, N.E., 'Is Outcome for Schizophrenia Better in Non-industrial Societies? The Case of Sri Lanka', *Journal of Nervous and Mental Disease*, vol.167, 1979, pp. 144–58.
11. Lo, W.H. and Lo, T., 'A Ten-year Follow-up Study of Chinese Schizophrenics in Hong Kong', *British Journal of Psychiatry*, vol.131, 1977, pp. 63–6.
12. Kulhara, P. and Wig, N.N., 'The Chronicity of Schizophrenia in North West India: Results of a Follow-up Study', *British Journal of Psychiatry*, vol.132, 1978, pp. 186–90.
13. World Health Organisation, *Schizophrenia: An International Follow-up Study* (Chichester: Wiley, 1979).
14. Sartorius, N., Jablensky, A., Korten, A. *et al.*, 'Early Manifestations and First-contact Incidence of Schizophrenia in Different Cultures', *Psychological Medicine*, vol.16, 1986, pp. 909–28.
15. Kemmerer, D.L. and Hunter, M.H., *Economic History of the United States* (Totowa, NJ: Littlefield, Adams, 1967).
16. Warner, R., *Recovery from Schizophrenia: Psychiatry and Political Economy* (London: Routledge & Kegan Paul, 1985).

17. Binder, R.L., 'The Use of Seclusion on an Inpatient Crisis Intervention Unit', *Hospital and Community Psychiatry*, vol.30, 1979, pp. 266–9.

18. Wadeson, H. and Carpenter, W.T., 'The Impact of the Seclusion Room Experience', *Journal of Nervous and Mental Disease*, vol.163, 1976, pp. 318–28.

19. Fortuna, J., 'Therapeutic Households', *Journal of Contemplative Psychotherapy*, vol.4, 1987, pp. 49–73.

20. Cashman, P., Herrick, M. and Levitt, R., 'A Team Approach to Treating Psychosis in the Community: Creating a Healthy Environment', *Journal of Contemplative Psychotherapy*, vol.5, 1988, pp. 117–32.

21. Fortuna, J., 'The Friendship House Project', *Journal of Contemplative Psychotherapy*, in press.

22. Stein, L.I. and Test, M.A., 'Alternative to Mental Hospital Treatment: I. Conceptual Model, Treatment Program, and Clinical Evaluation', *Archives of General Psychiatry*, vol.37, 1980, pp. 392–7.

23. Hawkins, K., *Unemployment: Facts, Figures and Possible Solutions for Britain* (Harmondsworth: Penguin, 1979).

24. Mosher, L.R. and Burti, L., *Community Mental Health: Principles and Practice* (New York: Norton, 1989).

25. Fairweather, G.W., Sanders, D.H., Maynard, H. *et al.*, *Community Life for the Mentally Ill* (Chicago: Aldine, 1969).

26. Backer, T.E. and Glaser, E.M. (eds), *Case Studies of Fairweather Hospital-Community Treatment Program* (Los Angeles: Human Interaction Research Institute, 1979).

27. Wansbrough, N. and Cooper, P., *Open Employment after Mental Illness* (London: Tavistock, 1980).

28. Warner, R., Taylor, D., Powers, M. and Hyman, J., 'Acceptance of the Mental Illness Label by Psychotic Patients: Effects on Functioning', *American Journal of Orthopsychiatry*, vol.59, 1989, pp. 398–409.

29. Timblin, P.J., 'A Statewide Consumer Organisation: U-Can-Du', presented at American Psychiatric Association Annual Meeting, San Francisco, 6–11 May 1989.

30. Sherman, P.S. and Porter, R., 'The Colorado Consumer Case-manager Aide Program', *Journal of Psychosocial Rehabilitation*, in press.

31. Patterson, C.J., 'Peer Counsellor on a Locked Psychiatric Inpatient Unit', presented at American Psychiatric Association Annual Meeting, San Francisco, 6–11 May 1989.

32. Leete, E., 'The Treatment of Schizophrenia: A Patient's Perspective', *Hospital and Community Psychiatry*, vol.38, 1987, pp. 486–91.

33. Hasher, R., 'Spiritmenders: A Client-operated Community Center', presented at American Psychiatric Association Annual Meeting, San Francisco, 6–11 May 1989.

34. Tepper, M.B., 'Tenderloin Self-Help Center: A Community Support Model', presented at American Psychiatric Association Annual Meeting, San Francisco, 6–11 May 1989.

35. Yalom, I.D., *Existential Psychotherapy* (New York: Basic Books, 1980).

36. Pattison, E.M. and Pattison, M.L., 'Analysis of a Schizophrenic Psychosocial Network', *Schizophrenia Bulletin*, vol.7, 1981, pp. 135–43.
37. Maddi, S., 'The Existential Neurosis', *Journal of Abnormal Psychology*, vol.72, 1967, pp. 311–25.
38. Fromkin, K.R., 'Gender Differences among Chronic Schizophrenics in the Perceived Helpfulness of Community-based Treatment Programs', unpublished doctoral dissertation, Department of Psychology, University of Colorado, 1985.
39. Dixon, L., Haas, G., Dulit, R. *et al.*, 'Schizophrenia and Substance Abuse: Preferences, Predictors and Psychopathology', *Schizophrenia Research*, vol.2, 1989, p.6.
40. Jones, M., *Social Psychiatry in Practice: The Idea of the Therapeutic Community* (Harmondsworth: Penguin, 1968).

'"I'm prepared to have him", said the headmaster, "but someone always vetoes his application whenever his name comes up for consideration at our board meetings." Someone always vetoes his application thought Joseph, and his mind addressed the treasured sanctum of a board meeting: someone always vetoes; someone normal; someone beautiful; someone blessed by normality; someone administering the rusty mind's rules of yesteryear; someone male — cigar-smoker perhaps; someone ruddy-faced with health; someone female — a skeleton in her cupboard, never give a sucker an even break; someone Christian worst of all, boasted ascetic, one of the head-strokers — poor child, God love him, ah God is good, never shuts one door but he opens another; someone genuine not able to bend the rules to match the need; someone satanic revelling in the sufferings of others; someone versed in the art of saying no; someone who had too many nos in their childhood; someone able to say no to a dumb cripple; someone always says no.'

Christopher Nolan, *Under the Eye of the Clock*

# 6
# Public Participation in Decision-Making
*Alexandra Lewis*

## Introduction

This chapter explores some of the conceptual and political aspects of public participation. The development of consumerism has reinforced the concept of public participation, over recent years. There is a variety of ways in which influence in decision-making can be exerted with a range of outcomes, at different levels in the processes. Current and future developments in welfare services in the UK, especially in the context of the health and community care recent legislation are intended to provide greater opportunities for a wider and more accepted public participation in decision-making, particularly for people with disabilities and their relatives and carers.[1] The development of a criteria for effective participation is especially important at this stage.

## Concepts

Understanding the concepts used in this chapter is essential, and a brief summary of these follow:

### The public

The public refers to people who are either active or passive members of communities, neighbourhoods, areas or the country as a whole, including people with disabilities. The public have a range of experiences and knowledge that can be a rich resource in deciding policy at all levels of decision-making. Some will have specific knowledge and group membership of national or local disability groups, others will have direct experience as users of services and carers, which will enable disabilities and relevant needs to be focused. The public have a vital role to play in the destigmatisation of

137

disability, by accepting the right of people with disabilities to live in the community.

## Participation

Richardson identifies participation as an old concept, fundamental to any democratic system. It is the method of expressing views to those in government, and to those with decision-making powers. Participation can be indirect, as in electing political or other representatives, or taking part in referenda, social surveys or pressure groups, for example. Direct participation takes place with elected representatives, officials and other decision-makers at specific meetings. Participation occurs in the process of decision-making and is not necessarily identified in the outcomes.[2]

## Decision-making

Decision-making is the activity and process of arriving at a decision. Usually this process is undertaken in a committee context. It is a major organisational activity particularly in the public sector.

### Influencing the policy process

There is a variety of ways in which the public can exert influence in the policy process, ranging from formulating public opinion to interest group participation and individual negotiations with decision-makers. Influencing public opinion can affect the demand for and development of social welfare. This can be seen in setting agendas, limiting choices and legitimising policies.[3] The climate of policy-making can be altered by public opinion, which has been moulded by media and political statements. Influence can be exerted at various stages of the policy process by limitation, formulation, decision-making, implementation or evaluation.[4] Apathy is taken to be implied acceptance, whereas positive and negative views are generally less open to interpretation. It is often more difficult for people with disabilities to take part in the political policy system, as many do not have voting rights or if they do have such rights, it is often impractical to use them. The increased use of postal and proxy votes can assist in encouraging participation in the political process but may also be open to manipulation, especially where these systems are used to assist people with disabilities. There is a need for all citizens and especially those people active in political parties in national and local government, to assist people with disabilities to vote. Most parties provide a collection and return transport service to voting stations but the service level will vary considerably locally. Greater effort and ingenuity is necessary in arranging access to voting, especially transport, for people with severe disabilities. Local and national politicians are likely to be more receptive to their constituents prior to elections, particularly when the margin between opponents is small. The level of assistance can therefore be as much a decision based on necessity, than on the principle of rights of people with disabilities as full citizens.

### Some theoretical approaches to the policy process

There are various theoretical approaches to explaining the policy process, of which pluralist views including a traditional and modern approach, will be considered as appropriate to US, UK, and many Western European systems. The traditional view purports that policy-making is widely dispersed, shaped by values and power within a more formal input process. It recognises that there is a gulf between citizens and political leaders in liberal democracies, resulting in some citizen apathy. The policy process is complex, variable and permeable by many interests. Political elites contest for votes on policy issues and control administrators to implement policies approved by interest groups in specific areas of citizen interest. Interest groups represent strongly held views on particular issues and provide government with information and more opportunities for consensus decision-making within a hierarchy of priorities. Citizens are able to have direct influence on policies via interest groups and informal contacts with government, enhanced by a decrease in parliamentary control and adversarial politics.[5,6] There is some bias, which can be explained by an overlap with elite theory. The latter, identifying the effects of increased specialisation and scale of organisations, results in decision-making with an oligarchy.[7] Such power may derive from people with political, economic and social positions, and can be exerted by taking decisions or non-decisions, maintaining the existing bias.[8]

Modern views about pluralist theory acknowledge the further bias in the system in an increasingly professionalised state, where government is a technocracy socialised by professional values which are seen as underlying the public interest ethos. There results a professionalisation of policy-making, transferring power in implementation to professionals. This can enable professionals to change policy implementation approaches, without changing policy or thorough assessment about the broader consequences that may follow. Elected representatives may decide to allow private agencies control over some policy areas.

### Preliminary obstacles to participation

Public participation may not be encouraged unless it is perceived as supporting professional aims. Closer relationships between powerful interest groups and professionals, and increased privatisation, may serve to contain public access to decision-makers.[9]

Citizen participation is an essential element of a pluralist system, as a means of promoting self-help, and a flexible counter to bureaucratic structures, operating separately or in tandem with state initiatives.[10] Such participation has occurred in the Community Development Programmes in the 1960s in the USA, and in Britain in land use planning, based on recommendations in the Skeffington Report.[11] Land use planning tends to result in public activities to ensure that the views of the affected public are known and that local interests recognised. Such activities have often been contrary to national policies and can adversely affect the move of people with disabilities into the community. The greater the stigma of the people moving into the community, the more the proposals for land use changes will be opposed, usually on the grounds that house values in the area will fall and citizens already resident will be socially and economically adversely affected.

### Consumerism

In parallel with these developments, consumerism has attempted to redress the balance of power between producers and purchasers of goods and services. This has now spread to the public sector, which is increasingly focusing on providing a high quality, valued service where goods managers know their customers and their needs and preferences. This knowledge can be gained by customer surveys, suggestions for service improvements, option testing, consumer panels, making standards explicit and listening to the customer.[12]

The subject of consumerism and the public sector was discussed in a recent article by Potter, and some principles to improve consumer access, choice, information, redress and representation in local authority and health services. Potter suggests that the political criteria used to decide access to services should be stated publicly, and access could be improved by decentralisation of services to localities. The elected or appointed representatives should know the consumers' needs and wants which can be incorporated into service performance measures. Proper methods to identify the needs of people who are unable adequately to express their views, need to be established. Consumers need to have information about services, policies and objectives to enable them or their representatives to exercise informed choice. Potter concludes that local authorities appeared to be more 'open' to people's views and opinions than health authorities.[13]

Potter's principles would, if implemented, empower consumers and the public generally, by making explicit information which could be used to improve the access to and accountability of public services. Some of this information is only spasmodically being made available to the public, and information services such as the Citizens Advice Bureaux, Consumer Advice Centres and Community Health Councils, are generally too overworked and underresourced, to assist the public effectively at the level Potter suggests. Neither local nor health authorities make sufficient information available about their services and the processes of their rationing access. Clearly, the more informed the public, the greater the demands for services and as resources are limited, the restricted information provided is therefore a rationing process on access to services. This rationing often works in favour of the more articulate middle class, which is consistently shown to obtain greater access to public services than, for example, social classes of unemployed and unskilled people. The health and local authority members are often from the more affluent middle classes, and to this extent may protect their own interests, and may not be knowledgeable about the needs and wants of their constituents and consumers.

Accountability is a word often used in terms of the proper provision of public services, yet the public often have great difficulty in establishing who is accountable and for what. If information to the public is increased, the ability of people to identify those responsible will increase. There is a clear further disincentive for more information to be provided. Potter provides an ideal for the public to work to, but the incentives to provide more information are very weak for those people holding the power in such authorities. Similarly, such power holders are going to be reluctant to devolve duties and decision-making, and improve access in that way.

Empowerment of the public is a potential threat to the existing system and is likely to be resisted by those people who benefit.

Redress mechanisms to process complaints and grievances can provide very effective quality control and general monitoring benefits. However, local and health authorities have generally not perceived complaints in a positive manner, both authorities being reluctant to publicise their complaints procedures. The 1985 Hospital Complaints Procedure Act in the NHS has been poorly implemented. There are Ombudsmen for both services, yet only the health service has open access for the public. The NHS has consumer representation in the form of independent Community Health Councils, whose secretaries are able to assist complainants in making complaints. Local authority members see this as their role for their constituents but are clearly not independent.

## A typology of participation

People can exert pressure on different authorities at various levels in the policy process, it is essential for people who may be involved to understand the methods used and the extent of involvement. A useful typology is provided by Arnstein, to enable people to realise the implications of a particular involvement in the decision process. The lowest level of participation is manipulation and therapy. Here, power holders, for example bureaucrats and professionals, involve the public in education exercises, which do not allow for effective participation. The result is often that the public consider that they have been spoken to rather than properly involved. This approach is common in the move of people with disabilities into the community. Sometimes the participation progresses to an exchange of information with interested parties, yet no guarantees can be given that policy changes will result. The next stage is placation, which allows advice and views of the public to be given to power holders, but the public are not involved in decision-taking and the advice and views may not be accepted. Public meetings to explain certain plans, such as changes to hospital services, tend to follow this pattern, especially in the current planning climate. In partnership situations, citizens and power holders can enter into negotiations in a series of trade-offs between the participants. This enables participants to decide priorities and to achieve some objectives and to accept some disappointments. This is the most common technique used, as there are usually resource and other constraints that result in changes in demands for both sides. Accepting second best or being pragmatic is a frequent compromise for people with disabilities. The alternative is often no action. The most effective participation is in delegation to citizens, control over decisions and management. This participation may occur as a result of the proposed changes in health and local authority services, as more voluntary organisations will be offered contracts to provide services for people with disabilities.[14]

This typology is important, as it focuses onto the complexity of public participation in decision-making, and the need for participants to understand the level of involvement otherwise expectations about the degree of influence that can be exerted can be unreal. When this happens, the effect is usually an adverse view of the power holders, by the citizens. If this occurs, it is often people with disabilities that are adversely affected, especially when they are moving into or living in a community that is hostile.

## Public knowledge of people and their disabilities

The long-term segregation of people with disabilities, from people who regard themselves as normal, has led to gross ignorance about the needs of people with disabilities. The British Education Act of 1981 has a clause which supports the integration of children with disabilities into the general education system. The debate around this Act has increased the level of awareness of the needs of children with disabilities, who will eventually become adults. The segregation of such children into special schools for specific disabilities, often encouraged by a lack of alternatives, has led to many children and adults not meeting people with disabilities in life situations.

Many people view the normalisation of people with disabilities into the community, now declared government policy, as unrealistic, as their lack of knowledge of the disability will prevent them from seeing the possibilities for these people to lead an ordinary life. Voluntary organisations and training centres, such as King's Fund Centre, that have led movement for change have also been viewed as impractical at times. There is a continuum of people with disabilities ranging from mild to very severe which the public tend to accept at the less disabled end and reject as the disability intensifies. Where people with disabilities have anti-social behaviours, and are often stigmatised, the public will frequently reject their presence in the locality, without listening to the case for normalisation to be made. The current trends of care in the community may thus be leading to the establishment of segregated institutions where integration for the residents is not made possible.

Professionals in services caring for people with disabilities may also support the views of the public in such cases, as often the responsibility of maintaining such people in the community can be very exacting and staff may hold similar undisclosed prejudices about their clients. Where local and health authorities do not work together, and with the private sector, opportunities for people with disabilities to share different experiences and activities can be limited. This may increase any segregation tendencies in the community. Many carers and relatives similarly view community placements with concern, sometimes based on fear of inadequate supervision of their person with a disability or based on their experience of inadequate or inappropriate services. Many people are stigmatised for example, as a result of their incontinence, which should not be a major problem. Yet, it may be the dividing line between home and limited institutional care, especially for elderly people. The failure of services to solve such problems adequately is the cause of much distress to the people concerned. There is a continuing need for public and professional education about disability as the policies for care in the community develop.

## Representing the interests of people with disabilities

Returning to theories of the state and the policy process, the concept of representation by elected representatives – in the institutional view, the only appropriate people to represent all constituents properly – raises some concern, given the low level of general public understanding of disability.[15-17] Such representatives at national and local level are likely to have personal experience of family and friends with disabilities, and either on specific or general matters will be effective representatives. Others may have developed a special expertise by interest group participation. It is extremely difficult for a person with disabilities to become an elected representative, and if elected, many democratic institution buildings have poor access and facilities for such people. Elected representatives in Britain are not campaigning on a direct disability mandate, unlike Italy, where mental illness became a cross-party political issue prior to the election. Subsequently, direct representation in the Italian Parliament enabled changes in legislation leading to policy changes for deinstitutionalisation from large mental hospitals, into the community.[18]

However, many elected representatives in British local and central government have contact with interest groups and professionals who have special knowledge of a variety of disabilities. It is then a matter of persuading their colleagues to support them in their aims. An example of the extent to which national representatives can achieve legislative change is the 1983 Mental Health Act, which was supported by national interest groups like MIND and MENCAP which represent people with mental illness and mental handicap respectively. MIND led a very long and hard fought campaign to improve civil liberties for detained patients in mental illness institutions. They also had support from professionals who wanted reform. These groups also supported Tom Clarke, MP in the progress of his Bill through Parliament in 1986, for better consultation and representation for people with disabilities.[19] In this example, legislation was passed by Parliament, but only a small part of the Act has been implemented to date. The reason for this lack of implementation is that current government politicians and the administration cannot accept the resource consequences arising from the Act, which gives more power to people with disabilities and their carers.

Influence on decision-making can be exerted in administrative departments, and taking the modern pluralist theories, interest groups have direct contact with professionals and administrators in the Department of Health, some of whom are members of specialist interest groups representing people with disabilities. Ministers, MPs, peers or senior civil servants from the department often take a major part at specialist interest group conferences, seminars and annual meetings. There is also cross-membership with members of the professional Royal Colleges. There are opportunities for a flow of information to and from the Department of Health which has the major lead in policy formulation and implementation via its field agencies in the regions and districts. This information tends to flow between oligarchies of relative representatives in interest groups and professional college leaders, a select group of people. Users and user groups are excluded as is much of the larger voluntary sector. The system is elitist and technocratic and an example of the modern view of pluralism in the policy process in operation.

NHS field administrative authorities have appointed members supported by professional specialists and administrators. Some appointees will be locally elected representatives, some will have interest group experience, others business skills. District health authority members have a duty to decide priorities of types and levels of services within national guidance and resource allocations.[20] There are differing perceptions of the members' role as they are not directly accountable to the community, but they are accountable for meeting their budget. Local authority members draw attention to their elected status on the local Council which they consider gives them representative status on health authorities.

Members tend to rely heavily on officers and often act as no more than a legitimation of officers' proposals.[21] Hayward suggests that health authority members have the opportunity to exert a significant influence on decisions if they recognise this potential. Successful participation depends on the perception of the chair and senior officers, and the role of members.[22] Recent research undertaken by Ham supports the role of members in practice to be the legitimation of officers' actions. The chair of an authority can have a significant influence on policy-making provided the officers, especially the District General Manager, since 1984, supports the views of the chair.[23]

This evidence suggests that people with disabilities need to ensure that their needs and wants are known to officers in health authorities, and for these to be placed on decision-making agendas. One way of ensuring this is to make direct contact with officers and develop mutual understanding of issues relating to specific disabilities and the services required. This can be done by individuals or, as in the pluralist theories, by interest groups, who will need to develop contacts with officers and service professionals directly at a variety of levels. Alternatively, representative and user groups may have direct access to planning services and assessing their quality in operation, via direct membership, cooption, or good working relationships with the local Community Health Council. The latter has a statutory representative role in the health service for the entire local population. For this representation to work effectively, Community Health Councils have direct individual and voluntary group membership and local authority members of their nominees, who aim to develop good working networks with the community and with officers of health authorities. This avenue of representation can be particularly helpful for very small representative and user groups often with limited skill, time and resources.[24]

### The future for representation in the health service

Health authorities, as currently constructed, and in the future after the changes in 1991 in Britain, are subject to criticism on the grounds that they are undemocratic and are not accountable to their local population. The reduction in membership after 1991, to no more than five non-executive members, will reduce the representation of broad disability interests to a very small scale. Other models for health authorities, in Italy and the USA for example, have directly elected and accountable members. However, these systems may result in over politicisation of health care, and underrepresentation of incapacitated and disabled people. Similar arguments are made against Community Health Councils in principle, and whilst their membership will not substantially change after 1991, their avenues of communication to and from officers and professionals in the health service may be substantially altered. It is as yet unclear how these changes will affect current practice and the representation for people with disabilities.

In the USA, a health care system that is being emulated in Britain, there have been patient representative programmes in general hospitals since the 1950s. These representatives have developed their role as experts who are able to put the patient perspective to professionals and managers in the hospital. Each patient has a personal representative whom he/she knows from admission. Programme directors are paid by the hospital and are assisted by volunteers who collate views of patients.[25] In Britain, Community Health Councils have a statutory function to represent the public and patients views in the health service. Members are non-professional lay people who are independent of the system. Links with the public and direct service users provide the information base for members to put these views to service and professional managers. In primary health care, general practitioners are encouraging informal patient groups to obtain the views of the practice patients about the services and to assist in making changes in the light of these views.

## Examples of public participation in health care in Britain

Britain is in principle a unitary state and the theory of public policy-making is that resource and service guidance for health care stems from the Department of Health, which attempts to ensure uniformity. In practice, as highlighted in research into the diversity of implementation of community care policy-making in four health authorities, there are substantial differences in progress and comprehensiveness of policy implementation. Multipurpose territorial departments, as in Scotland and Wales, have a greater capacity to develop coherent services and financial policies than the Department of Health.[26] On closures of long stay hospital provision, England led in making rapid reductions in in-patient beds. This process has been slowed recently by the current government as a result of pressure from the National Schizophrenia Fellowship and SANE, which led an effective campaign about the lack of adequate alternative services and facilities in the community. Demands to keep people in hospitals until resources are made available to develop alternatives have been heeded. Some aspects of this campaign are discussed in Chapter 7. The research suggests that diversity is not acceptable but inevitable. In other countries, diversity is seen as a positive aim, allowing for a range and variety of services and facilities and providing more flexibility and innovation opportunities.

### An example from Wales

In Wales, the Welsh Office has developed a strategy for service development for people with a mental handicap which provides an interesting case study of planning with carers and users at department and Regional level and implementation locally.[27] The Secretary of State took a leading role and as a result there was wide consultation and implementation. Throughout the process, consumer participation in the planning and management was encouraged and carer's involvement emphasised. The objective of the strategy was to develop integrated and comprehensive community services for people with a mental handicap. Resources were set aside specifically for this strategy. A Central Planning Group was set up, consisting of six professionals from social services, education and health authorities, with six lay people coordinating the local district representation, plus a member from a non-mental handicap voluntary body to provide a broader voluntary organisation link with other community support. The main consumer involvement was at the local level, where carers and front-line workers met in open forum making decisions which were forwarded to the Central Planning Group.

The All Wales Strategy is an exceptional example of public participation at the highest level. This has continued informally in the localities and involves user groups like People First, so that the direct needs of users can be identified and met. The formal participation continued in the All Wales Advisory Panel which had representation from MENCAP and SCOVO, the voluntary organisations for people with a mental handicap and others with a broader range of experience.

There were several specific factors that led to the degree of participation in this strategy. First, MENCAP had formed a strong Welsh group and had become an effective, credible force, in Wales. Secondly, informed public and relatives were concerned at the waste of health and local authority resources, and they wanted to ensure better decisions were made. Thirdly, there was concern that the Welsh Office was developing its own plans without consultation with interested parties. At this point MENCAP enlisted the services of a sympathetic M P who had knowledge of mental handicap issues, having relatives with the disability. Together, pressure was put on the Secretary of State for Wales to intervene and to ensure that a high level of participation was allowed.

Experiences of consumer participation in this strategy were monitored as a research project funded by the then Department of Health and Society Security. Carers had a variety of experiences during this project, many of which are common to participants in other contexts.

First, many participants lacked adequate knowledge about the strategy, about the planning process and about how they should participate. All these skills are essential for participants to have credibility and to be effective members of planning groups. It is essential that supporting voluntary groups assist participants to gain the skills necessary, and the Community Health Councils may be able to assist from their experience of performing such functions. Professionals in the services need to help participants in planning forums to understand the system and their role in the process before the discussions begin. The People First participants and other user groups needed such help and support to be able to make their views known. Participants that I have met from user groups have usually developed considerable knowledge about talking to bureaucrats and professionals and getting their views accepted. Advocacy and self-help schemes may also assist in enabling users to be better communicators of their needs and wants. Some of these schemes are referred to in Chapter 3.

Secondly, active carers found the time required to participate unrealistic to their caring role, and some left. Others found the whole process too laboured with little practical results for them, so they lost interest. Others still found the whole process of committees slow, boring, intimidating and frustrating. Many were apathetic and left others to provide the representation, leaving a nucleus of the same people appearing on different committees, who often dominated meetings and who had become quite professional and rather aloof from the rest of the carers. People attended as individuals rather than representatives of organisations. Service professionals and voluntary groups need to ensure that there is sufficient provision of financial or carer support to enable proper representation at such planning meetings. Too often, it is the experienced committee participant who dominates and reduces the ability of less confident participants to be effective. Had people been explained the process and the length of time before any results would be seen, their expectations would not have been raised unrealistically.

Thirdly, both carers and professionals became frustrated by the different views about service priorities, the latter often being accused of causing delay to urgent schemes for carers. Differing perceptions of priorities for services is a common outcome and often results from both sides not understanding each other's constraints and experiences. However, where services are to meet the needs of users and their carers, it would not be unreasonable to take many of these priorities as paramount, based on the actual experiences.

Finally, the length of time taken to draft the consultation plan left very little time for broader views to be gathered from relevant parties. This left some people feeling that they had not had sufficient opportunity to express their views. There is no doubt that to consult widely takes an enormous amount of time. It would appear that the level of participation of interest groups and users was considered to be high and therefore the broader consultation would be less necessary. This is not usually the case.

Interestingly, the Welsh Office did not repeat this participative approach for the All Wales Strategy for people with a mental illness, but did allow a period of six months consultation on the draft plan. This raises a question as to whether the mental handicap participative exercise principle will ever be repeated.

### Patient participation in primary health care

Patient participation in primary health care has been a developing area for the last decade. Progress has been slow but steady and the focus has been on general practice. Some general practitioners have welcomed the development and a National Association for Patient Participation was founded in 1978 as an umbrella organisation for local groups, with some Department of Health and King's Fund support. In a recent study of these developments, Richardson and Bray consider the climate of consumer participation has provided the credibility.[28] The movement has been encouraged by Community

Health Councils from whom local group organisers have received considerable support. The objective of participation in primary health care is to provide health education and promotion to enable people to take a greater control over their lives and their health, and to improve local services in cooperation with doctors and their team. There is a two-way exchange of information between practice staff and their patients which provides for a more responsive service and a sense of ownership to the consumers.

Sixty-three local groups were identified in Scotland, England and Wales, in 1987, and of these, more were in town and rural situations rather than urban areas. Local nationally affiliated groups at 1990 number 130 – a rapid rise. Support has been given directly by the Royal College of General Practitioners, which in 1983 set up a Patient Liaison Group of seven doctors and seven lay members to provide a forum at national level to disseminate views and information on matters of mutual concern. Some Regional Patient Liaison Groups have followed the national model.

Patient Participation Groups have been growing in number across the country, and the reason for this is that people wish to help themselves and their doctors. The majority of people only see general practitioners for their health care, and thus there is a greater ease of understanding the service aims, and contributing to these aims is less stressful and stigmatic than within the hospital services, especially psychiatric services. There have been visible achievements in purchasing equipment, changes in the operation of practices, provision of information booklets for self-education, meetings to educate the public, supporting self-help groups and visiting and transport schemes. One of the most difficult problems with these groups is the management of relations between the practice providers and group members. Over or lack of involvement by doctors can be a fundamental problem that needs to be addressed. The importance of the national association to support participants in some of their difficulties cannot be overemphasised. Where the groups work responsibly, and staff appreciate their good intentions, there is much to commend.

The importance of patient participation groups in general practice could become greater as the implications of the Health Service White Paper become better known. The direct budget holder in general practice, in particular, will need to ensure that they are meeting the health and service needs of their patients, and potential patients. The groups may also undertake a protective role for people who have chronic illnesses and/or disability who may not be especially welcome as they are high resource users for the practice. I envisage further encouragement nationally and locally to set up such participation groups, encouraged by the practice professionals.

## Public participation in the hospital services

It is almost impossible for an individual to influence health authority members or offices, however extreme the individual's health needs. There are examples where local interest groups have directly influenced authorities to provide services often after a public outcry over the lack of services, or poor quality of those provided. Many such organisations reflect the views mainly of carers rather than particular individuals. Larger organisations tend to be accepted as legitimate for involvement in service discussions, leaving smaller, lesser known groups with little chance of representation. In some cases, such as the mental health services in Nottingham and Newcastle, ex-users are encouraged by supportive managers to organise ward meetings for current service users, and to withdraw when the groups are self-maintaining, as discussed in Chapter 3.

Often, user and smaller groups will not enjoy such support and need to be aware of opportunities to sue the statutory bodies to represent the public in the health service, a function of their Community Health Council, which can effectively ensure that views of minority groups and individuals can be brought into the service at points of delivery, and in the policy-making process. Community Health Councils were set up in 1973, in the NHS Reorganisation Act, with a broad monitoring, complaints and planning remit in the NHS. Taking the example of CHCs in England and Wales, there is usually one CHC for each health district whose membership is composed of local authority councillors and nominees, voluntary organisations and appointed individuals. Most councils belong to a national association which coordinates views and issues from member CHCs and relays these to relevant bodies, including the Department of Health and ministers. Where appropriate, the association lobbies Members of Parliament of all parties on particular health matters, and especially at times when health legislation is being debated, as with the NHS and Community Care Bill in 1990.

Community Health Councils seem to be under almost constant criticism for their unrepresentedness, as they are composed of mainly middle-class, middle-aged, white members. What is usually ignored is that they often have members with a range of disabilities and are able to coopt members with special knowledge to assist them as required. Where, regretfully, CHCs on the whole have been unsuccessful is in attracting members from a variety of minority ethnic groups, often because they do not accept the CHC role and procedures and the relevance of these to their health issues. CHCs important function is to develop knowledge of the health needs of their local population. If this is undertaken properly, all organisations and users should be aware of the opportunities that the CHC provides to ensure that authority members, officers and professionals in the health services are aware of the wants and needs of local people.

CHCs also have an excellent record of representing the needs of people with a variety of disabilities who may not be able to represent themselves. In their monitoring of health services, CHCs have often identified service failures in long-stay services, such as poor food, dirty and unpleasant environments, lack of access to holidays, lack of effective therapies, few opportunities for employment and low staffing levels. Publicity about the poor level of services for long-stay residents, especially elderly, mentally ill and mentally handicapped people at local and national levels has led to pressure to develop alternative care, and closure of inappropriate services. Most CHCs take their role in planning services as a priority, and it is by active participation in this planning role that local groups and individuals with particular knowledge of disabilities can contribute effectively.

The future role of CHCs is unlikely to be changed substantially as a result of the current legislation on health service changes. However, there may be modifications to limit their participation in some parts of the new structures of health services, especially those where more managerial independence is proposed.

## Participation by voluntary organisations

Voluntary organisation participation straddles health and social services providing services and information. Financial support for charities and voluntary organisations is usually paid on an annual grant basis by health and local authorities. Decisions on grant funding are mostly made by officers with authorisation by members. The process may be informal or formalised via the system of joint finance.[29] The latter provides for voluntary organisation representatives to take part in the decision-making process at the Joint Consultative Committee of health and local authority members and officers, about the allocation of specific finance to fund care in the community projects. In practice, there has been some dissatisfaction with this process as the two authorities have taken a short-term view of such expenditure and have largely supported capital rather than revenue expenditure, providing facilities rather than services. The representation by elected voluntary organisation members has not been a success because many people have found the task difficult due to a lack of knowledge about broader matters other than their own specific interests. Sometimes the voluntary members have come from the same organisation, usually the larger organisations that are well known to the authorities. This process is to be changed as a result of the White Papers and the new process has yet to be made explicit.

Health authority support given to voluntary organisations and charities was £33 million in 1987 − 8, and has been increasing at a substantial rate each year. Taking the average value of payments, hospice and terminal care took 65 per cent, children and child abuse 27 per cent and mental handicap and care attendant organisations took the main share. The future relationships between health, local authorities and voluntary organisations are likely to be substantially changed in the implementation of the changes proposed in the two White Papers, where authorities will be encouraged to purchase services from private and voluntary bodies in a contractual relationship.[30] There is considerable concern on the part of voluntary organisation members that this will create a dependency that will be difficult to break and will substantially alter their ability to be advocates on behalf of the people that they claim to represent. If this does happen then there is likely to be a proliferation of smaller non-direct care service providers, who will wish to represent particular interests and who may find that difficult in terms of access to decision-makers and funding. The development of interest group and user's consortia and forums, as for example in the London Boroughs of Camden, Islington, Harringey, Lambeth and Westminster, may be a possible trend for the future. Alternatively, a division of larger voluntary organisations into advocacy, information and service sections may occur to provide clear separation of functions. Organisations such as MIND, MENCAP, Age Concern, and the National Schizophrenia Fellowship are developing user group sections, but they largely represent the views of carers and relatives rather than direct service users.

## Participation in local authority planning

Local authorities provide a major part of the services required for people with disabilities, including finance, access and transport, education, housing, day and residential services, meals-on-wheels, respite care, and other support services. They also hold the land use planning function except for the exempt land owned by the NHS.[31] Members of local authorities have joint membership of health authorities and cooperate over joint financial projects with health, for care in the community. The level of success is dependent on the coordination of policies between the two authorities and the ability of officers and members to work together.

There is no independent consumer representation, members consider that they were elected to represent the range of views and interests of their ward constituents. Links can be made with local organisations representing people with disabilities, and members with social welfare interests often become social service committee members responsible for welfare services. Most of the policy planning is undertaken by officers with members contributing at draft policy stage. It is therefore the officers that need to be influenced by people with disabilities to enable their needs to be actively considered. Resources are constrained at national and local levels and tend to be used in priority for statutory services, for example, child care, and less for adults with a disability as they are not generally protected by legislation to the same extent.

The poor implementation of employment opportunities, incomplete implementation of the 1970 Chronically Sick and Disabled Persons Act, and the Disabled Persons (Services, Consultation and Representation) Act 1986 support this view. In March 1987, four clauses of the latter Act were implemented. Local authorities have a duty to consider the needs of people with disabilities and their carers, to provide information about services that may be relevant, to coopt people with special knowledge of the needs of people with disabilities onto councils, committees and other bodies. In many local authorities where there is good cooperation with people with disabilities, carers, voluntary and statutory bodies, and commitment on all sides to ensure needs are met, then imaginative schemes can be developed. In Newcastle, the local authority wanted to develop a Metro local train system that could be used by everyone. They set up a variety of consultations with a range of potential users at various stages of planning and constructed a pilot train and station to enable users to comment on the ease of use. The result is a system that can be used by all the public with a minimum of difficulty. In Exeter, the closure of large psychiatric hospitals has led to the development of jointly planned community residences. In the London Borough of Camden, the Link scheme has developed community housing for profoundly disabled people in the community. Sometimes the joint chairmanship of health and local authorities has speeded some of these developments.

## The Birmingham project

Birmingham City Council launched a three-year Community Care Special Action Project in January 1987. It had two major aims: to devise and implement corporate strategies for community care, using the full range of Council and other agencies, and to develop methods to involve consumers and their carers in auditing, planning and development of community care services. The project was concerned with changing the culture and process by which the services for people with special needs are planned, managed and delivered. Developments to involve service users have included asking assistance from them to give their views on the relevance and quality of services provided. They will also be involved in providing guidance and advice and in developing policy. This intense involvement of service users and their carers gives them a sense of being valued.

The outcome of the project has been to identify the poor public awareness of the needs of carers, a general lack of understanding of disability, and negative views about the potential of people with disabilities. Many solutions to problems identified by carers were not expensive, but were alternative ways of delivering services more sensitively and flexibly. Officers and members of the Council have had direct contact with service users and their problems with the Council services. The project has linked up with some innovators in the community who have offered their support for the aims. It has provided an injection of some short-term goals into the service which may stimulate longer-term changes. The improvement of coordination between departments and agencies has been preferred rather than structural changes of the department, and as a result better working relationships have developed between health and social services and users of services.[31]

This type of exercise takes a great deal of courage to launch, but the reward of a more substantial involvement of users and carers in service planning and provision, at a level that participants can feel is useful to both providers and users, can be greater understanding about the services provided and required. This project is generally in line with the increasing orientation of local authorities to consumers, and with the requirements of the 1986 Disabled Persons Act.

## The Avon experience

An earlier series of pilot projects undertaken by Avon Social Services in the early 1980s took a different approach to develop closer cooperation between social workers and volunteers in the community. This was consistent with recommendations made in the Barclay Report in 1982[32] and the previous Seebohm Committee in 1968. A research project undertaken by the Department of Health into community care, in 1981, identified the importance of informal carers, who were a valuable resource for social services to harness.[34]

Seven schemes were initiated including information packs for people with a mental handicap and their carers, and a variety of other resources to help people understand the disabilities and to obtain appropriate help. The provision of home care assistants for people with a variety of disabilities, living in their own homes, involved some training and a complex management of volunteers to ensure that expected cover was always available. A scheme was devised to provide funds for volunteers to take local elderly people on outings and to purchase coal for heating, via a series of road wardens. Schemes for short-term residential care with families in the community were negotiated for children and elderly people. The remainder were for pre-school day care and stroke rehabilitation in the community. All the schemes were assisted by voluntary organisations and the social services department, with social workers working with volunteers, carers and users in the community.[35] The Avon social services schemes show how the advantages of greater public and user participation and joint statutory and voluntary cooperation provide better and more relevant services and a more varied choice for people with disabilities and their carers, enabling the statutory services to increase the range and type of services available without substantially raising the costs of the services to consumers and the local population. The new proposals in the White Paper for community care suggest that the future of social service welfare services will be undertaken as in the Birmingham and Avon examples. As health authorities are no longer to concentrate on providing services, so local authorities are to have an enabling role and less direct service responsibility.

## The future for public participation in the welfare policy process

Public participation is a complex subject conceptually and practically, and how it relates to the decision-making process is fundamental to enabling people actively to determine their current and future lives. The context of participation is within the role of the state and the policy process discussed in this chapter is taken to be the modern pluralist theoretical stance. The context needs to be understood to provide the opportunities for participants with this information to direct their efforts productively. There is a variety of options to be considered when deciding where influence should be exerted from elected representatives, professional social and economic elites, interest groups and bureaucrats. The climate of opinion, which is media influenced, determines the acceptability of public participation at any time. The general approval of consumerism reinforces the legitimacy of public participation. State policy with respect to disability has developed to accept normalisation as a key aim. However, this has been a limited exercise as many people with disabilities are economically weak and their families often suffer various levels of poverty. The fiscal crises in the Western world have encouraged more community participation in care activities, as the provision of professionalised services at the level required would prove to be economically and politically unacceptable. This leaves the opportunity for a variety of bargains to be struck between people with disabilities, their carers, and professionals and administrators involved in welfare services. The ultimate aim should be to have a participative role that delegates responsibility to people who are directly affected and their carers to ensure that services are provided for and by them to meet their needs. The current reluctance of the British government to empower people with disabilities with relevant finance, to enable them to purchase their own services, suggested by Lady Wagner,[36] is confirmation of a view of partial integration of people with disabilities into the community.

The general level of public misunderstanding about the needs of people with disabilities is a major problem for moves to enable them to participate in decisions about their life needs, and for normalisation to be a high priority. There will be a need to provide good education programmes and access for people with disabilities to participate in work and social activities with people who do not have the same problems. The more difficult part of this educative process will be to develop understanding about people who are disabled and who have socially unacceptable behaviours, who will eventually live in the community. This lack of general understanding seriously affects the ability of many representatives of the general public to represent adequately the needs of people with disabilities. It can also limit the acceptance of these people into the community.

The examples of participation reviewed show clearly the benefits that can accrue to all parties involved, and to the population generally. The most important constraint will be the acceptance by the professions of the deprofessionalisation of social welfare. This may be an inevitable consequence of the difficulties now experienced in the recruitment of sufficient school leavers into many professions. There is a possibility that the resources unused in providing professionals could be made available to fund voluntary and informal care in the community.

Effective participation requires a general political acceptance that such activities will be encouraged. Participants must be seen to be credible, either by the democratic process or by agreement that they have a knowledge that is required in the process. If the participants are elected or appointed they need to be aware of the needs and wants of the people they purport to represent. This is also the case of people in interest groups which are composed mainly of relatives and carers, rather than service users and people who have disabilities. Any public participation exercise requires good information for participants about the issues being considered, and about the system of participation and the variety of expectations of probable outcomes. Options about possible trade-offs between participants need to be identified as the process progresses. Where voluntary participants are involved in participatory processes, great efforts need to be made to ensure that any expenses are met, including costs of additional care, transport, relevant skill learning, interpretation, etc., so that people with practical knowledge can take a full part. Whilst it is appropriate for planning to take place in small committees, it is important that full consultation over an accepted time period is undertaken to consider wider views. The advantage of engaging in what is often considered to be a long and laborious process is that services will meet the needs of those for whom they are to be provided, and will be robust to criticism.

The future development of participation has been established in legislative principle and requires the practice to be widened. The NHS and Community Care Bill which became law in the summer of 1990, in Britain, will authorise health and local authorities to develop service-purchasing roles and to contract for services with other statutory authorities, the private profit and non-profit sector, and with voluntary organisations. In theory, the consumer is to have more choice in the services and the quality available. However, it remains to be seen how it will work in practice. Orientation of services to consumer preferences should encourage greater participation in the planning and provision of welfare services. Yet the independent status of self-governing hospitals and some general practices could reverse this trend. The key issue is likely to be the adequacy of resources available for health and community care services to enable variety and choice for users and their carers.

## References

1. Department of Health, *Working for Patients*, CM 555, (London: HMSO, January 1989); Department of Health, *Caring for People*, CM 849, (London: HMSO, November 1989).
2. Richardson, A., *Participation* (London: Routledge & Kegan Paul, 1983).
3. Whitley, P., 'Public Opinion and the Demand for Social Welfare in Britain', *Journal of Social Policy*, vol.10, no.4, 1981.
4. Lassawell, H., 'The Decision Process', in Polsky, N. (ed.), *Politics and Social Life* (New York: Houghton, 1963).
5. Dahl, R.A., *Modern Political Analysis* (Englewood Cliffs, NJ: Prentice-Hall, 1983).
6. Dunleavy, P. and O'Leary, B., *Theories of the State* (London: Macmillan, 1987).
7. Michels, R., *Political Parties: A Sociological Study of the Oligarchical Tendencies of Modern Democracy* (New York: Dover, 1959).
8. Barach, P. and Baratz, M., *Power and Poverty* (Oxford: Oxford University Press, 1970).
9. See 6 above.
10. Hatch, S. (ed.), *Mutual Aid and Social Health Care*, Association for Researchers into Voluntary action and Community Involvement (London: Bedford Square Press, 1980).
11. Skeffington, A., *People and Planning: Report of a Committee on Public Participation in Planning* (London: HMSO, 1960).
12. Stewart, J. and Clarke, M., 'The Public Service Orientation: Issues and Dilemmas', *Public Administration*, vol.65, no.2, 1987, pp. 161–79.
13. Potter, J., 'Consumerism and the Public Sector: How Well Does the Coat Fit?', *Public Administration*, vol.66, no.2, 1988.
14. Arnstein, S., 'The Ladder of Participation in the USA', *Journal of the American Institute of Planners*, 1969.
15. Simon, H.A., *Administrative Behaviour: A Study of Decision-making Process in Administrative Organisation* (New York: Wiley, 1947).
16. Simon, H.A. and March, J., *Organisations* (New York: Wiley, 1958).
17. Lindblom, C.E. *The Intelligence of Democracy: Decision-making through Mutual Adjustment* (New York: Free Press, 1965).
18. Ramon, S. (ed.), *Psychiatry in Transition: British and Italian Experiences* (London: Pluto Press, 1988).
19. Disabled Persons (Consultation and Representation) Act 1986 (London: HMSO, 1986).
20. Department of Health and Social Security: Health Service Circular, 7/77, 1977.

21. Regan, D. and Stewart, J., 'An Essay on the Government of Health: The Case for Local Authority Control', *Social Policy and Administration*, vol.16, 1982, pp. 19–43.

22. Hayward, C., *Policy Making in the NHS* (London: Macmillan, 1981); Hunter, D., *District Health Authorities in Action*, (Birmingham: Birmingham Health Service Management Centre, 1985); Hunter, D., 'Managing Health Care', *Social Policy and Administration*, vol.18, 1987, pp. 41–67.

23. Ham, C., *Managing Health Services: Health Authority Members in Search of a Role*, SAUS Study 3 (Bristol: Bristol School of Advanced Urban Studies, 1986).

24. Klein, R. and Lewis, J., *The Politics of Consumer Representation: A Study of Community Health Councils* (London: Centre for Studies in Social Policy, 1976).

25. Society of Patient Representatives of the American Hospital Association, *Essentials of Patient Representative Programmes in the Hospitals* (Chicago: American Hospital Association, 1986). p. 1,251.

26. Hunter, D. and Wistow, G., 'The Paradox of Policy Diversity in a Unitary State: Community Care in Britain', *Public Administration*, vol.65, no.1, 1985.

27. McGrath, M., 'Customer Participation in Service Planning – the All Wales Experience', *Journal of Social Policy*, vol.18, part 1, 1988.

28. Richardson, A. and Bray, C., *Promoting Health Through Participation* (London: Policy Studies Institute, paper no. 659, 1987).

29. Department of Health and Social Security, Health Service Circular, 7/77, 1977.

30. Ibid.

31. *Community Care Special Action Project* (Birmingham, Snow Hill House, 1990).

32. Barclay Report, *Social Workers: Their Role and Tasks* (London: Bedford Square Press, 1982).

33. Seebohm Report, *Report of the Committee on Local Authority and Allied Personal Social Services*, Cmnd 3103 (London: HMSO, 1968).

34. Department of Health and Social Security: Report of a Study on Community Care, 1981.

35. Harbert, W. and Rogers, P. 'Community Based Social Care: The Avon Experience', Occasional Paper 4 (London: National Council of Voluntary Organisations, 1983).

36. Wagner, G., *Residential Care: A Positive Choice* (London: National Institute for Social Work / HMSO, 1988).

# Part III
# The Test Ground: Turning Principles into Policies

# Introduction

The final chapter concentrates on the translation of normalisation principles into policies, and unless we get the policies right, we will continue to come across the following descriptions:

> There is now ample evidence as to the patchy and uncertain nature of carer support. Simply obtaining help can be a major problem . . . nobody sees it as their responsibility to give information to carers. As a consequence whether or not they find out about services is largely an accident.[1]

> The average long stay patient's life is dominated by hospital routine to the point where loss of self-esteem, interest in life and even leaving take over. The institution takes over.[2]

These two quotations from the same page of a recent British social work journal highlight how far we are at present from implementing the principles of normalisation into everyday policies and services. Nevertheless, Chapter 7 illustrates also how much has already been put into effect, in areas as diverse as education, employment, networking, deinstitutionalisation, and alternatives to hospitalisation along the road to revalorising the life of people with disabilities. In so doing, examples already discussed in the previous chapters are utilised, as well as some new illustrations from different countries and across the range of client groups.

The gap between what has already been put into effect and what remains to be done is explored by indicating the complexity of planning and implementation, and the difficulties of which policy-makers are aware, as well as those of which planners are either unaware or prefer to remain unaware. Policies are important as a summary of social intentions, as a beginning of putting principles into practice.

This book is also a summary and an analysis of the current state of the art, pointing out the realistic potential of people, policies and services which is yet to be achieved. Hopefully it will stimulate future efforts to ensure a valued life for people with disabilities.

## References

1. 'Poor Support for Carers means Indirect Rationing', *Social Work Today*, 3 May 1990, p.6.
2. 'Mental Health Care "Inhumane"', ibid.

'But at that time, perhaps nobody will want any longer to compare anything awful to cancer. Since the interest of the metaphor is precisely that it refers to a disease so overlaid with mystification, so charged with the fantasy of inescapable fatality. Since our views about cancer, and the metaphors we have imposed on it are so much a vehicle for the large insufficiences of this culture, for our shallow attitude towards death, our anxieties about feeling, for our reckless improvident responses to our real "problems of growth", for our inability to construct an advanced industrial society which properly regulates consumption, and for our justified fears of the increasingly violent course of history. The cancer metaphor will be made obsolete, I would predict, long before the problems it has reflected so persuasively will be solved.

The controlling metaphors in descriptions of cancer are in fact, drawn not from economics but from the language of warfare. Every physician and every attentive patient is familiar with, if perhaps inured to, this military terminology.'

Susan Sontag, *Illness as a Metaphor*

# 7
# Policy Issues
*Shulamit Ramon*

## 1 Normalisation and social role valorisation in the context of current social policy

### 1.1 Why now?

Ideas concerning the right of people with disabilities to an ordinary life have been proposed as policy directions in the recent past throughout the Western world, with the introduction of the deinstitutionalisation principle as part of community care policies. However, only in Denmark and Sweden have the principles of normalisation and SRV become part of official policy.

As already mentioned, both concepts appear in professional writings from the end of the 1950s in the Scandinavian countries; by the end of the 1960s in North America; during the 1970s in Australia; and only from the 1980s in the UK. By now it has become fashionable for politicians, too, to talk about normalisation, empowerment, and self-help. We need to ask why these ideas appeal to politicians across the political spectrum.

The answer does not lie in an upsurge of interest in people with disabilities per se, despite the increase in the number of people with disabilities who live longer today in each of the industralised countries. Estimating the number of people with disabilities throughout the different Western countries is not simple: most countries publish figures per disability, and use somewhat different criteria for evaluating the degree of disability. Nevertheless, the existing evidence suggests that a range of between 12 to 17 per cent of the general population of Western countries has a disability.[1] Translated into people, it means 6 million in Italy, 7 million in the UK and roughly 20 million in the USA. A recent survey of people with seriously incapacitating disabilities has put their number at 3 million in the UK.[2]

The appeal of normalisation, empowerment and self-help seems to be related to current concerns with the 'crisis of the welfare state'.[3] Doubts as to its achievements and viability have come to the fore from the beginning of the 1970s, neatly coinciding with the oil crisis and the economic recession which followed it.

The viability and desirability of the welfare state have been criticised on the Right by those who accept the monetarist argument. For them, the provision of universal services by the state through taxation is not only wasteful, but also dampens people's motivation to improve their own wealth and that of their society. In the name of individual freedom, it is argued that people should have the right to choose services and control them by having buying power.

The shortcomings which most observers would identify as typical of state services — too much bureaucracy, impersonal service which lacks sensitivity to individual needs — are seen by monetarists as inevitable within a state-controlled system. The failure of welfare provisions to eradicate poverty and ill health is attributed within this approach to the inevitability to do so. At the same time, the desirability of such an eradication is questioned.

The criticisms of the welfare state from the Left relate to the delivery style of services, to concerns regarding the continuity of care and quality assurance, the degree of choice, and the issue of preventive policies which could eventually lead to a substantial decrease in poverty and ill health, if not to their full eradication.

Both critiques share the belief that post-war welfare systems have largely failed to offer services which prevent chronicity, enable clients to choose, and are aimed at meeting individualised needs. Meeting these three objectives is at the core of the normalisation approach.

Self-help[4] is also attractive to those who wish to reduce state intervention and who assume that it will be a less expensive service because those who offer it would not be paid. It is much less attractive to those who either disagree with the idea of cheap labour and/or are concerned with the need for a comprehensive service available at all times, in which self-help can be at best only one component.

The road from self-help to reliance on volunteers and on informal carers as the main carers for people with disabilities is superficially logical, as historically people always cared for their kin, and women did so more than men. Yet it is a preference which does not take into account the changes in women's lives and ambitions, or in the structure of the nuclear family. Opting for the private sector, with its non-profit and its for-profit components, is based on the wish to encourage the taking of responsibility by groups in the community. It is assumed that a smaller agency will offer a more personalised, yet less bureaucratised service at a reduced cost, and that people are more motivated if they work for profit. This is a very mixed bag and its echo within the normalisation approach is also mixed. Self-help would form a natural sequence of SRV in a society which encourages mutual support. However, all the other permutations mentioned above are not so 'natural' and require careful consideration. In this climate of opinion it should be stressed that curtailing bureaucracy, having a small and user-friendly service, and a very limited exploitation of informal carers have been the hallmarks of the Scandinavian welfare systems, which invariably do not have a voluntary service tradition but have instead a state provided system. They also happen to be the countries where the normalisation principle is more developed and applied in practice.[5]

Normalisation seems to be closely linked to the failures of the welfare state and the potential resolutions of it which are offered from both sides of the political spectrum. However, the precise relationships between these solutions and normalisation depend on their ideology and the meanings attached to the normalisation principle.

Unlike normalisation, empowerment and self-help, social role valorisation has not become a slogan used by politicians or policy-makers. Some suggest that it is a meaningless term; others that it is too complicated, cumbersome, and removed from a commonsense understanding of life.

*Consumers' power*
This has become a much discussed issue, again used as a slogan by politicians of contradictory ideological convictions, as discussed in Chapter 6. To date, neither the majority of people with disabilities nor their informal carers have enjoyed much of such a power. Informal carers are not even considered as consumers of welfare services because they are not the carriers of an identified disability. For although the term 'consumers' originated outside the realm of welfare services, its meaning within that domain is conferred by pinpointing a handicap: to have a need implies being handicapped. For informal carers to be seen as having the right to support, social attitudes concerning the stigmatised role of being a recipient of any service need to change radically, rather than attitudes to caring.

The needs of people from ethnic minorities which are not met as part of a service require a specific policy brief, raising the issue of whether a separate service is the answer or not. Following the logic of integration, multiracial and multicultural services would be preferred within the normalisation conceptual and ethical framework. Yet such an position could lead to policies and services which are 'colour-blind',[6] in adhering to the 'natural' stance of following the wishes and needs of the majority rather than paying specific attention to those of minority groups. At the same time, the focus within the SRV approach on respecting individuals should include also respect for their cultural preferences.

### Policy-making

Books have been written about the processes of policy-making, summarised neatly in the title of one of them as that of Choice, Change, and Conflict.[7] Hopefully, yet another C can be added to this list, namely, Challenge.

Most policies are made public, with legislation heading this list in terms of the seal of formal approval. Below references will be made to relevant legislation in which policies related to normalisation have been outlined.

## 2   Normalisation and SRV policies

The role of policy-makers is to implement the intentions of the public, as expressed by its representatives, into structures and strategies that put intentions into practice. In the context of normalisation this would imply designing policies aimed at deinstitutionalisation, social role valorisation, and opportunities for ordinary living.

The task is enormous, if not outright impossible, as it encompasses individuals' life-spans and those of families, different types of disabilities and within each of them, varied levels of abilities and difficulties in functioning, different professional disciplines and variations in social context. All these need to be considered if the hoped for continuum of care is to materialise.

### 2.1   Deinstitutionalisation policies

It is appropriate to begin with deinstitutionalisation policies because these have predated the formulation of SRV in its present form, taking place as part of community care policies. It is also a policy which has been attempted in every Western country.

In most societies, it took the form of a declaration of intent, followed by administratively proposed policies which were not based on a process of consultation with either professionals or users and informal carers. In some countries, there is evidence to suggest that they were influenced by the thinking of a small circle of professionals.[8] The planners saw their task as providing a less restrictive environment which resembles more ordinary living, yet secures the containment of people whose behaviour is seen as offensive or dangerous, and retaining the asylum function which total institutions were supposed to provide initially. This list reflects the everlasting duality of care and control. With the exception of Italy, the main impetus for deinstitutionalisation has come from governments keen on the closure of large and financially crippling institutions, assuming that services in the community will cost less, using professional support for legitimation purposes.[9]

Given this motivation, there was concern as to how to close an institution and transfer its residents to other facilities with minimal fuss and costs, yet within the implicit boundaries of a socially acceptable mode of conducting this process.

Resources in this context were primarily the available budget and buildings. People – be they residents, staff, families or communities – seem to have mattered much less. As part of the transfer process, the assessment of levels of dependency of residents was conceptualised and carried out by professionals commissioned by the planners. A number of roles and relationships which are central to the SRV approach have not been even considered within these assessments. Exceptions do exist, mainly in the field of mental handicap, where assessment schemes already influenced by the normalisation approach have been put into operation.[10] In the various versions of the 'getting to know you' instrument, the emphasis is on getting to know the person with a disability as a person (and significant others) rather than focusing on the disability, in a relatively lengthy yet informal process. In 'circles of support' the focus is on the contribution by each member of the circle, including the person with the disability, to meeting identified needs jointly.[11]

Similarly, little attention was paid to the abilities or wishes of the workers in the institutions to be closed. In some cases, the principle of redeployment was established as part of management and trade union negotiations, but rarely in terms of the needs of an institution in a process of deinstitutionalisation. Staffing requirements for the new facilities were calculated separately, primarily based on the assessment of dependency levels and the assumption that residents would live outside, grouped by a similar level of dependency as the main criterion.

I would argue that – with the exception of the 'getting to know you' and 'support circles' schemes – these policies are at best only tenuously related to the normalisation principle or that of SRV. More often than not they perpetuate the prevalent approach in the institution where the assumption is that the residents' inabilities are the inevitable reflection of their disabilities, and where little attention is paid to their potential.

The policies also fail to take account of the institution as a living organism, and as the framework which has to change for it to resemble ordinary living. Such a change is necessary if the residents and the staff are to be prepared for this new living and work style. In a number of cases, attempts to prepare residents for life outside were merely an appendix to the main policies. Professionals were allowed to prepare users in small groups in terms of self-care and social interaction skills, as a special programme which was unrelated to the rest of their everyday life in the institution.

The lack of attention to the need to change the institutional framework and the focus on residents' inabilities derives first from the strong belief that hospitals should not be closed, because they are the best provision for a population deemed as largely incapable of living outside a total institution. Secondly, it is rooted in the overemphasis on the new settings, without much attention to the inevitable relationships between the two sets of the same organisational system.

The Italian experience demonstrates a different approach to this issue.[12] The change was treated as a process in which residents, staff, the organisation, and the general public are the participants. The focus was on modifying the internal structure of the institution to enable the mirror image of ordinary living to take place inside it. That image was not the one embraced within therapeutic communities, which may have a therapeutic value but only in part simulates ordinary living. The initial planning took the form of an agreement between a regional administration, the trade unions and a group of professionals working in an institution. The day to day planning, implementation and replanning took place in the daily communal meeting of residents and staff, as well as in smaller *ad hoc* groups. Thus the process of planning was part of the changing institution. This was possible primarily because the professionals who were running the institution were committed to changing and dismantling it. The financial arrangements were also more simplified than in the American or the British context, as the initial costs were met by the hospital administration, all resources saved by the closure of a ward being transferred immediately to the transition requirements of the organisation; no new workers were hired initially but they left when the residents moved out; and the separation between the health and social services (usual in the Anglo Saxon world) no longer existed in the field of disability.

The process entailed not only the shedding of power by doctors and nurses, but also the gaining of new expertise and satisfaction in an area of work where stagnation was in evidence previously. The different approach to planning is perhaps best illustrated by the fact that sites were not sold despite the fact that many of the old hospitals were on urban sites, but were used instead for communal purposes, often for a combination of mental health with ordinary communal facilities (e.g. a children's nursery, a secondary school or a riding school manned by ex-patients).[13]

The Italian mental treatment law of 1978 is unique in legislating an end to new admissions to existing psychiatric hospitals and in forbidding the building of new hospitals after an agreed date. However, even this law leaves the alternative services unlegislated.

Although Psichiatria Democratica developed in isolation from the literature on normalisation, its focus on deinstitutionalisation, on ordinary life opportunities, and especially on the dignity and citizen's rights of users, closely resembles the SRV approach. This reinforces the view taken here of the inherent similarities in the delivery system of welfare services for people with disabilities in terms of both problems and solutions within the First World. The main departure lies in the more collectivist approach adopted by the Italians to understanding and working with users, staff and the community. This difference from Anglo Saxon and Scandinavian societies stems from operating in a specific social context, rooted in a different set of political beliefs and an understanding of the political dimension in the field of disability.

The failure of 'traditional' deinstitutionalisation policies has been documented, usually in terms of failing to ensure a reasonably dignified and safe life in the community, rather than in terms of looking at what has happened to the institution and its inhabitants, be they residents or staff. Yet the transfer of residents from one total institution to another surely has to count as failure within the normalisation framework. Such transfers have taken place in the UK and the USA.[14] They make a mockery not only of the idea of ordinary living, but also of basic respect and choice. The attempt to justify such moves as offering the 'least restrictive environment' to users may be correct in some instances. On the whole, it would reflect the lack of commitment to deinstitutionalisation.

The need for asylum for some people (both ex-residents and the so-called 'new long stay') is a more serious argument for retaining non-institutionalised residential establishments. Yet most of those who call for asylum do not demonstrate that they have considered options other than a traditional hospital setting, despite the existence of evidence to illustrate that crisis centres and refuge facilities can cater for this need without the additional disadvantages of the traditional hospital.[15]

Cedar House in Boulder, described in Chapter 5, offers one such convincing example. Mental health centres with beds, as they exist in Trieste where only sixty-four compulsory admissions have taken place between 1978 and 1988 (all of them in an open setting), provide another useful alternative.[16] Instead, in many cases, planners have gone for the simplest option, namely, that of adding beds in the general hospital. This leaves unanswered the question of the usefulness of such beds beyond the very acute stage for asylum purposes, let alone for normalisation goals.

Likewise, current calls to reopen total institutions, because of a higher rate of homelessness and imprisonment among people who suffer from mental distress than in the general population, come from those who assume yet again that this group becomes homeless and imprisoned because of the disability, and not because of the lack of suitable support and services in the community. This argument continues to be voiced even by those who should know better, since they were around when people came from the American psychiatric hospitals and lived in sheltered accommodation for years until these were sold off to developers, who evicted the ex-patients, turning them *then* into homeless people.

### 2.2 Social role valorisation

Together with integration, social role valorisation is the ultimate goal of normalisation. Its implementation depends on policies for deinstitutionalisation and opportunities for ordinary living. On the surface, it is a tricky objective to plan for as it cannot be measured or provided for quantitatively. I would argue that most planners and professionals are not used to considering SRV as an integral part of their work and therefore are less prepared to include it – implicitly and/or explicitly – in new policies than the components of deinstitutionalisation and opportunities for ordinary living.

In the following section, policies will be examined as to how far they advance 'the social role of persons or groups at risk of social devaluation, via the enhancement of their social image and their personal competencies'.[17] Wolfensberger suggests that such an enhancement can take place within physical settings, relationships and groupings, activities, language and other symbolic images.

The ENCOR programme which covered all of eastern Nebraska is one of the most comprehensive attempts.[18] As the Danish parents association demonstrated a decade earlier,[19] the Nebraska project illustrates how parents can turn their sense of inferiority and stigma, as well as their frustration at the lack of adequate services, into a crusade aimed at changing attitudes, policies and actual services. In the process of doing so, the organisation itself went through different phases, such as mounting a moral crusade, lobbying, advocacy, planning, delivery of services, monitoring, and training. An industrial consortium was created, harnessing the local business community to offer employment opportunities to people with learning difficulties. The parents demonstrated the ability to move from one phase to another, to use existing resources to the utmost (e.g. the existing law of the right of people with developmental handicap to free public education until the age of 21), and to engage professionals' support. The latter deserve some of the credit for the success of the programme, and for being able publicly to express the following:

> Underfinancing of public institutions is the problem. Public zoos spend more to care for a large animal than is spent to care for the average retarded resident in our institution. While five of the largest zoos spend an average of $7.00 per day to care for their large animals, average expenditures for the mentally retarded in Nebraska institutions is approximately $4.50 per day. In many ways we treat the retarded like animals. Retarded persons who could be trained to eat independently, to use the bathroom, and to wash, clean, dress and groom themselves are often sentenced to living in untrained conditions and to waste away without attention.[20]

The achievements of the programme are impressive in terms of preventing chronicity, the utilisation of ordinary services which have become sensitive to the needs of this group of people, and improving their quality of life in the process. The programme included working with urban and rural populations, with those suffering from a severe degree of such a handicap, as well as from a combination of different disabilities.

Although there seems to have been considerable public support for these changes, much less is known as to whether the social image of people with developmental handicap and that of the parents has changed, and in what direction, perhaps because of the preference for quantitative proof. An element which has developed more in the 1980s, but missing from this programme, is that of the direct users' voice, choice, and their participation in the service.

A different type of social role valorisation is offered by the various types of brokerage, some of which were described in Chapter 2.[21] The principle of these schemes is that the control over the financial resources, and the final say concerning hired support, is in the hands of the person with a disability. Often this person would hire one worker to coordinate the package of services required, but the ultimate control will be retained by the person with the disability. This enhances social role valorisation because of the social value attached to financial control, to choice, and to being an employer.

Opportunities in which people with disabilities can provide a positive contribution to other individuals or to the community are those in their self-image and social image are enhanced. Such opportunities vary from simple friendship and mutual support to self-advocacy, voluntary and paid work, and creative artistic activity. The examples of the Nottingham patients' council (described in Chapter 3) and of the counselling service offered by ex-users in current users in San Francisco and Oakland (see Chapters 3 and 5) highlight the ability of ex-patients to provide a valuable support to people currently suffering from mental distress. The participation of residents in the process of selecting future workers mentioned in Chapter 2 is another example of a policy aimed at SRV, which can be put into effect with little investment but which requires the preparation of both the staff and the residents, and symbolises a changed mentality in both.

The Chesterfield Mental Health Project, where the director of the project also manages the community centre in which the project is located, offers an interesting variation on the theme of SRV and that of integration. There representatives of the users' group of the project sit on the central management committee, as do the representatives of all the other (ordinary) groups which use the centre regularly.[22]

Finally, a glaring example of how to sabotage the goal of SRV may be useful in highlighting the type of barriers which SRV policy-makers have to take into account. In the first few months of 1989 a series of posters appeared in many bus stops, railway stations and cinemas in London. These invariably portrayed a dark and distorted face with captions such as: 'He thinks he is Jesus . . . you fear that he will kill you . . . they do not want to know . . .' At the bottom of the poster, in small letters, one could read: SANE – Schizophrenia A National Emergency, with a postal box and an address to write to. The organisation behind this campaign of inciting fear and defamation consists of parents of people who suffer from schizophrenia and doctors who oppose the closure of Britain's large psychiatric hospitals. They have as their patron none other than the heir to the British throne, Prince Charles, and are receiving considerable donations from well-known millionaires. After the intervention of users' organisations and MIND, the advertising board has advised the removal of the posters. The British press, free as ever, refused to publicise the criticisms addressed at SANE, and it remains to be understood why Prince Charles should be its patron. What is not in doubt is the blatant attempt to downgrade the social image of people who may suffer from schizophrenia, a group of people not noted for enjoying a socially valorised image. This mixture of inflaming public fears and prejudice in the name of care and compassion is of doubtful benefit to all of us.

### 2.3 Policies concerned with opportunities for ordinary living

The thrust of this endeavour has been aimed at people who left institutions or who are in the process of doing so. Policies targeted at the prevention of institutionalisation and segregation within the community are coming more to the fore in some areas (e.g. children with physical and mental handicap), but are still absent in others (most notably in relation to mental distress).

Ordinary living includes housing arrangements, education, employment, leisure, income, use of welfare and cultural services, self-care and social interaction abilities.

The last two elements are the preconditions required from the person with a disability as the entry ticket to ordinary living. Policy-makers have viewed such retraining as a professional domain. Professional providers may offer the most suitable methods of such a preparation, but are they the best judges of standards for ordinary self-care and social interaction? On the whole, the specific programmes which are in operation cater for skills which are so basic as to make this question seem rhetorical. Yet at times the fuss over issues such as not making the beds in the morning reminds the observer that many ordinary people either do not make their bed in the morning, or do it in a way which leaves a lot to be desired in terms of neatness. As with adopting a child, where the standards required of adoptive parents are considerably higher than those demanded from natural parents, re-entering society does not seem to be a natural right, but has to be re-earned by those who have been institutionalised.

The more this process can take place within ordinary environments, the better from the perspective of SRV. Yet doing so calls for greater flexibility and risk-taking by the trainers.

*Housing*
This is a natural and essential requirement for leading an ordinary life. Planners seem to warm to it more than to other areas of ordinary living, perhaps because of its concrete expression and the sense of power which controlling it gives; more than once houses have been bought by planners and people's needs have had to fit in with the property.

For a variety of reasons the majority of those who leave the institutions cannot – or should not – go back to their original home. Alternatives include hostels, adult placement schemes with land-ladies, group homes, core and cluster arrangements, small nursing homes, and independent living.[23] Each of these can be run as a commercial enterprise or as a public or voluntary scheme. In a number of Western societies housing for this group is progressively dominated by the commercial sector, with central government encouragement, as a way of cutting down public expenditure. This has implications for quality assurance which will be discussed in section 4 below.

Looking at these housing arrangements from the normalisation perspective, independent living would be the most fitting solution. Yet with the exception of nursing homes all other possibilities could enable residents to lead a life similar to the ordinary style. This would imply that standards of privacy, division of labour, separation of living, working, education and leisure spaces, control over finance and shopping, would be kept mainly as they would be in an ordinary home. These are not expensive demands, but they mean that the level of staff control is minimised, individualisation is maximised, and expectations of a uniformed, regimented, lifestyle are left behind. The pronounced gap between the ideal and the real which can be observed in the majority of housing settings for people with disabilities is apparent because of the combined effect of residents' disabilities and the lack of staff and facilities to enable a more individualised lifestyle. Planners are, on the whole, uninterested in the lifestyle of the residents, and see their task as completed when people move out and have a roof over their head. The more protecting that roof is, the better from their point of view, because this is seen as securing the containment element and reducing the risk of potential harm to oneself and others. Usually, the more protecting the establishment, the less ordinary and the more institutionalised it becomes. Warner, in Chapter 5, has outlined a number of interesting alternatives for this group.

When asked, users opted to live on their own, i.e. in the most ordinary style.[24] Yet most of them are not living in this way, nor are there plans to enable them to do so in the future. This brings us back to the issue of the threat experienced by planners, professionals, the informal carers and the public of the users' right to fail in their bid for autonomy which was mentioned in Chapter 1. By not being given the right to fail, users are not being given the right to succeed in a more autonomous way of living. It also raises the important yet neglected issue of how to support people with disabilities who live on their own. The support circles scheme provides an interesting example of how this can be done in the case of people with severe physical disabilities.[25]

Evaluation of the range of arrangements mentioned above is highly complex and biased by the fact that it is impossible to predict how individual residents would have fared in another housing setting.[26]

Supporting people with disabilities who opt to live with their family of origin would be an integral part of the normalisation approach. This implies supporting also the informal carers through respite care, adapting generic services to cater also for the special needs of these groups (such as schools and health centres). Family support schemes and paid home carers have been introduced in more than one country, and seem to be working reasonably well when attention is paid regularly to the needs of the people with disabilities and the related needs of their family members.[27]

*Education*
This has become a universal service for children, backed by legislation in all Western societies. In some countries, the right for free public education for people with a disability is extended until the age of 21.[28] Countries differ in providing special and/or integrated education, the level of support given to individual children in order to sustain their educational achievements, the length and type of pre-entry assessment, and after school hours and holidays provision. As a rule of thumb, countries with an emphasis on nursery education offer more services, and more of the integrated kind, to children with

disabilities, and have less elitist, privatised, educational systems. While in Britain the debate as to the advantages and disadvantages of special education continues, it has become a non-issue in the countries which have attempted integration on a large scale. From the perspective of the normalisation approach, the advantage of integrated education considerably outweigh those of special education, since only integrated education can offer social role valorisation and attitudinal changes by the majority of ordinary children, parents and teachers. This does not contradict the need to pay attention to individualised needs within integrated education.

The educational and social achievements of children with disabilities within ordinary schools have rightly been a source of pride and optimism for all those involved in this process. So have been the numerous innovations invented along the way, to sort out the no less numerous difficulties which spring up in education normally.

Elena was a 10-year-old girl in a wheelchair, unable to talk and write normally, whom I met in an ordinary school in Arezzo.[29] She has learned to communicate through magnetic letters and numbers assembled on a board small enough for her to handle. Observing the sheer pleasure with which she welcomed the teacher's praise for her correct answer to a mathematical problem, when her turn came, was an unforgettable experience for me. Had she had been to a special school, Elena would have perhaps reached the same intellectual attainment, but would have been unlikely to sense the appreciation of ordinary children, or enjoy their company. Remaining at home meant that her parents and siblings had to provide her with considerable support, and their sense of achievement would have been much curtailed had she been to a special school, let alone away from the family.

Children's education seems to be the service with which parents are most satisfied, even when it is in a special setting, and where they feel involved and treated with respect.[30] Is it because education is a universal service, where people are not treated as objects of scientific injury? The education of adults with disabilities has received much less attention than that of children as a policy issue, in the same way that ordinary adult education receives scant attention when it is not directly vocational. However, here too there are attempts at providing education within ordinary further education settings, frequently in the form of tailor-made courses, but also by joining ordinary classes which contribute to the sense of being socially valued (see the example of college credits given to ex-users trained to become case manager aids, in Chapter 5).

*Employment*

Employment, namely paid work, is a crucial aspect of ordinary living in a society where people are judged mainly by what they do for living and how much they earn. It figures little in policy terms for people with disabilities, reflecting the assumption that most people with a long-term disability are unfit for ordinary living.

Warner has illustrated that there is a greater interest in the economic productive capacity of people with a disability during periods of economic affluence.[31] Yet there is little to demonstrate that this interest has led during those periods to policies focused on an active search for employment for people with disabilities. Several countries have legislation which ensures quotas for the employment of people with disabilities in large working places. However, the proportions are so small that they cater at best for a tiny minority. From the viewpoint of normalisation, it is doubtful whether such legislation is the way forward as it perpetuates taking people into employment as disabled, rather than because of their specific ability. Tudor describes the history and the problems of one such law in Italy.[32]

Several interesting and reasonably successful approaches to the issues of assessing the current and potential abilities for employment of people with disabilities, of preparing them for employment, and finding a job have been tried out in various Western countries.

High street shopfront employment agencies currently operating in London provide one interesting example of the value of up-marketing employment opportunities for this group.[33]

Workstations in industry have been operating in the USA since the 1950s, demonstrating that it is possible for people with disabilities to train and work alongside people without them. In Italy, and now in the UK, there are a number of work cooperatives in which people with a disability have an ordinary job, but within the framework of a supportive group and a more flexible time schedule than in an ordinary post.[34] Although most of the cooperatives are fully managed at the beginning by professional staff, gradually the managing responsibility is shared with the associates. Work cooperatives are an arrangement used by people without disabilities in Italy, where the largest and most successful cooperatives of people with any disability can be found. As with housing, it is easier to find employment opportunities for people with a physical or developmental disability than for those who suffer from long-term mental distress, though evaluation studies demonstrate that success in employment is unrelated to symptomatology.[35]

The empathic understanding of other people with a disability can be utilised as one ability in locating, training, and employing service users, provided it is not used to segregate current and past users from the rest of society. The care manager aids scheme in Denver[36] (briefly described in Chapter 5) highlights the advantages of such a scheme, but also the potential disadvantages. The latter include paying people with a disability less than others.

*Leisure*

This is accepted as a legitimate activity for adults who earn their living, or who can afford it, and for children. Thus unemployed people express a sense of inferiority and shame when they use concessionary rates in a leisure complex, while pensioners do not. Socially valued leisure activities can enhance enjoyment, sharing in ordinary activities, and self-image, as well as offering a rewarding mode for skills training and creativity. The more integrated within ordinary environments such activities are, the better. Paradoxically, people who move from their homes to residential facilities seem to be more cut off from both integrated and special leisure opportunities,[37] due to lack of attention by policy-makers and direct providers.

Policy-makers take account of leisure activities in budgeting for holidays, for example. However, all other such activities come under the heading of 'therapeutic activities' and depend on the attitude and initiative of specific agencies. The more an agency is committed to the normalisation principle, the more likely it is that leisure will be targeted as an integral activity which offers choice and empowerment to the users. An interesting example is provided in a Jewish Day Centre in North London where the centre attenders share in the planning of a wide-ranging entertainment programme provided for five afternoons per week.[38]

*Income*

Policies aimed at securing a minimum income for people who are not employed and those on low wages form a central part of national social policies. The majority of people with long-term disabilities are recipients of these policies. More than ever before, the sums paid by central and local government are less than sufficient to cover the cost of a dignified, ordinary life. In the case of people with disabilities, this adds to their suffering, reduces their level of control over their reality, and makes a mockery of the normalisation principle. This state of affairs is related to the monetary approach to welfare, where the reduction in benefits is aimed at making people less dependent on the state. Whatever the merits of this argument in general, it misses the point in relation to people with long-term disabilities who are unable on their own to become less dependent financially. In fact benefits are structured in the opposite direction, penalising those who attempt to work on a part-time basis instead of encouraging them, by reducing their benefits considerably after reaching a ridiculously low level of earned income.[39] The recent introduction of the poll tax, in April 1990, in Britain has also led to the reintroduction of registering people as 'severely disabled' for the purpose of being exempt from paying 80 per cent of the tax. This reinforces stigmatisation and the sense of inferiority. The stigma attached to receiving most of these benefits adds insult to injury in the case of people with disabilities and their informal carers. Parents of severely physically disabled children, interviewed by Glendenning,[40] expressed their relief at being able to claim, and receive without being means tested, the British attendance allowance. This example illustrates that it is possible to minimalise the stigmatising effect.

## 4  Quality assurance

Attention to and developing adequate mechanisms to secure the quality of services is a necessary ingredient of good policy-making. At the formal level it is most developed in the USA, perhaps as a spin-off of the attention in the commercial sector to effectiveness and the existence of mechanisms for the involvement of a large number of citizens in local government. In a number of countries, there are currently attempts to legislate compulsory assessment of people's needs in the community prior to discharge from an institution (the Schizophrenia After Care Bill proposal in the UK), or for such an assessment to take place in the community (the Canadian Vulnerable Persons Act, the British Disabled Persons Act 1986), as a measure of quality assurance. The emphasis on assessment runs the risk that while resources become available for assessment, these are not necessarily channelled into services designed to meet the needs which the assessment highlights. Most policy-makers are trained to build in means of ascertaining cost and managerial effectiveness primarily. Traditional evaluation by professionals of a service tends to focus on individual users and programme outcomes, rather than on the process by which outcomes were attained.[41]

Within the normalisation approach the *process* is at least as important as the *outcome* if not more, due to the material and symbolic significance of the mode of delivery as a form of social valuation. Therefore, the quality assurance schemes developed by SRV protagonists concentrate on the degree of implementation of the normalisation principle and its values, which necessarily include also measures of administrative and cost effectiveness.[42]

For example, integration is looked at in terms of physical and social instances, appropriateness refers to age-appropriate interpretations and structures, possessions, labels and forms of address, sex behaviour, personal appearances. Quality of setting relates to physical comfort, environmental beauty, individualisation and interactions.

As Mike Lawson describes in Chapter 3, this evaluation takes place in a group which consists of professionals, users, and community representatives, all of whom need to become partners to quality assurance processes. Tyne has outlined how the process of evaluation can spearhead awareness of and commitment to normalisation, provided participants are aware that quality assurance does not come instead of normalisation policies and practices.[43] Within the ENCOR programme there were several suborganisations which ad different quality assurance functions.[44]

A different type of quality assurance is required in the British Home Registration Act of 1984, whereby a local authority has to register a privately run home for people with a disability to secure the quality of its provision. The local authority also has the duty to inspect such establishments periodically, but in fact apart from withdrawing registration has little powers to make home owners improve what is on offer.[45] Given the chronic shortage of staff in these authorities and the relatively low priority attached to these duties, it remains unlikely that the task will be carried out properly without it being funded by central government. This highlights the cost element of quality assurance and the necessity to bear it in mind in policy decisions. The issue of inspection will become more prominent in the British context, as according to the White Paper, *Caring for People* (published in November 1989), local authorities will have the duty of inspecting not only residential facilities, but all services for people with disabilities.

## 5   The economics of normalisation policies

Costing normalisation policies must rank high on the list of policy-makers' nightmares. Central and local government exert pressure to reduce costs; consumers organisations and professionals exert the pressure in the opposite direction. In addition, what to cost and how to go about it is not as clear cut as it may appear to the unsuspecting observer. For example, housing, education and food stamps (an American benefit, which enables the use of vouchers for food only) are often not included in the cost analysis of the health services policy-makers, as they are not part of the health element of the budget.

Bearing in mind the need to cost the continuum of care, and the different needs of different client groups, the overall budget has to include a variety of residential settings, use of generic and specialist health services, the cost of domiciliary support, support of employment, educational and leisure activities, and income maintenance. Within each of these items there will be more than one option, and hence each option requires to be costed. Cost-benefits and cost-efficiency are important parameters to be kept in the background of these calculations, as would be the role played by central and local government, the public service sector, the not-for-profit and the for-profit sectors.

For systems in transition, as during the process of closing large hospitals and establishing alternatives to hospitalisation in total institutions, Glennerster and Korman[46] proposed the need to calculate three additional types of cost:

— transaction costs; namely, management time and energy in maintaining the momentum of change;

— compliance costs; financial inducement to collaborators in the process of transition to ensure that their services will not suffer during the transition period and to secure their cooperation;

— transition costs; of maintaining the services about to be closed at a reasonable level of quality. While some of the cost of running them will be reduced as the process of closure accelerates, some unit costs will be in fact increase (e.g. nursing costs cannot be calculated per patient).

To these items the cost of establishing new facilities and individualised residents' programmes has to be added.

The realisation of the 'invisible cost' has led economists, and some governments, to propose that the cost of supported living in the community for people who have left institutions is not only not much cheaper than hospital life, but may be even more expensive.

However, available costing which includes the hitherto invisible costs continues to demonstrate that living in the community is cheaper, even with a considerable degree of support. Stark, McGee and Menolascino[47] have demonstrated that over a period of fifty-four months the difference in cost between living in an institution ($74,219 at the beginning of the 1980s) and that of being supported by ENCOR ($52,972) is $21,247, for severally mentally retarded people. The cost of gradually moving to live at home with support leads to a further reduction ($18,211). Warner (in Chapter 5) provides another illustration of a community setting for people in an acute psychiatric crisis. Although labour intensive, the overall cost is cheaper than that of hospital beds.

Shiell and Wright provide a thorough account of the costing of residential care for children with a profound mental handicap, in a recent British project.[48] Their conclusion is: 'This cost data appears to substantiate the hypothesis that care in the Project is initially more expensive than a place in a larger community unit but that these costs can be reduced in the longer term as children are placed in foster care' (ibid., p.263). However, Glennerster and Korman (quoted in reference 48) are proposing that care in the community is more expensive than hospital care for adults with mental handicap.

Yet Beecham and Knapp, in the latest detailed study of costs of reprovision of people from psychiatric hospitals, illustrate that the average cost of living in highly supported settings in the community is still cheaper than that of hospitalisation.[49]

Different countries have opted for different financial arrangements with which to provide resources for the change in the services catering for people with disabilities, and by now there are some lessons to be learned as to the relative advantages and disadvantages of these mechanisms. For example, the US federal government has not financed the whole cost of the transition process, but did provide seed money for new services outside the institutions as early as 1963. This has proved to be very beneficial initially, but also to be a rather unstable source of finance some years later because of its high dependency on the changing ideologies of the US government.

The British government has for a long time resisted any national sponsorship of either hospital closure or new community facilities, preferring to encourage and follow requests for joint health and social services funding, which worked with varying degrees of success.[50] From the point of view of a local authority, there are major drawbacks in joint funding, as the authority is expected to finance fully such initiatives after the first few years. A 'dowry' system has been worked out by the British government for the purpose of financing the moving out of long-term hospital residents. For taking on the responsibility of settling him/her in the community, each service is to receive a one-off sum, varying between £12,000 to £20,000.[51]

It was mentioned above that the main financial incentive in the Italian case has been the possibility of immediate transfer of money and workers from sections of the hospital to the community. The use of case managers who budget and purchase services is now brought into the British system, more than a decade after experimentation with such schemes in the USA,[52] where mixed financial results have been reported. The underlying assumption is that the budget holder is cost-conscious as well as need-conscious. This may work if indeed the system is need-driven rather than cost-driven. Holding and distributing a budget may conflict with the advocacy role of care managers, may colour their assessment of needs, and their role as quality assurance inspectors.

The Canadian states of Alberta and British Columbia (and by now also Grampian region in Scotland) opted recently to fund brokerage systems (described in Chapter 2), which offers greater flexibility in the use of resources and user's control over service providers.[53] This could be seen as another version of case management.

From the perspective of the normalisation approach, the brokerage arrangement is the most cost-beneficial in securing a high degree of client's choice and control. It is too early to know how cost-efficient this system is, but it is likely to minimalise the administrative costs. Yet it is the antithesis of the ethos of generations of planners in Western societies where large is still beautiful. Moreover, ensuring that brokers are indeed providing what they are contracted to do, and that the services their clients-cum-paymasters need are available in the community, is no mean task for the future generation of planners. Cost requires to be seen as a dependent variable, as the outcome of underlying ideology of policies and the form of organising service delivery. Instead, many governments – and economists – would like us to believe that it is an independent factor.

## 6  Policies aimed at facilitating organisational innovation

In a way, all the policies outlined above are concerned with organisational innovation since they are aimed at changing the existing situation by creating new organisational structures.

However, very few of the policies illustrate that their makers are familiar with, or take into account, the dynamics of innovation, its initiation and maintenance beyond the superficial level.

In the actual process of planning, a number of obstacles to good planning and implementation came to the fore.[54] Primarily these included:

1.  Lack of coordination and proper consultation among the different agencies involved in the process. This was based on the assumption of the subordination of the other participants to the planning process, as well as the belief in the uniformity of the desired solution.

2.  Lack of adequate mechanisms for the necessary financial support from central government towards the cost of the transition elements in the planning (see also section 5 on cost).

I would add to the list the following:

3.  Investing in motivating workers to approach the change in a positive light, and providing them with ongoing backing, is of central importance to the success of innovation. Examples include the training offered by the King's Fund and David Brandon in Britain, by John O'Brien in both the USA and the UK, and the deinstitutionalisation work in Italy (described in section 2.1 above).

4.  The difficulties reported when pioneering programmes were in the USA, and in any major organisational change,[55] illustrate yet again that a mechanical, purely administrative approach to innovation is doomed to failure. Yet when the takers are allowed flexibility and expression of their own originality there is a better chance of implementing the spirit of the original innovation.

5.  Barrier analysis tends to consist of mapping financial and physical barriers to change. Instead, it has to include potential power brokers who may oppose the innovation, how to disarm them and how to enable most losers from the change also to gain from it. For example, special education teachers lose their base when a special school closes down. Yet if given a role in planning the integrative service and the new types of support which it will require, most of them would be likely to become enthusiastic converts.

6. The lack of more than lip service consultation with users, informal carers and the local community often results in either adopting the wrong policy or coming up against considerable obstacles. Planners tend to view such consultations as a waste of their time, as a cumbersome process which will unearth conflict instead of the blanketed consensus which they are after. They are correct in assuming that genuine consultation will make their administrative task more complex. They are, however, wrong to believe that by avoiding it the potential of intentional and unintentional sabotage of their objective has been overcome. It must be tempting for planners, as for politicians, parents, and teachers, to impose change. Unfortunately, for real innovations in human services to be accepted, issues have to be argued time and again, demonstrations made, examined, and modified, and as many people as possible involved in the process. Moreover, consultation with users and informal carers can be unpleasant and time-consuming, as the latter may be expressing their pent-up anger, only some of which would be directly related to the specific planning initiative. Yet only through a consistent process of consultation, which includes providing users and informal carers with tools for a rational debate, can this difficulty be resolved.

   Some protagonists of the normalisation approach believe that communities should be not consulted, as is the case when non-institutionalised people move into a neighbourhood. From the few existing British examples in which the attempt to consult was also an attempt to involve users' organisations and ordinary people in the deinstitutionalisation process, my conclusion would be that while this was a demanding process, it proved its worth in short- and long-term outcomes. This is also the message from the All Wales Strategy for people with learning difficulties, described in Chapter 6.

7. The decision as to which sector to use in specific components of the normalisation process is of crucial importance, but is neither clear cut nor easy to reach in a number of cases. With the increase in the availability of services offered by different sectors (i.e. the public − (including central and local government) − the private for-profit and the private not-for-profit), the planners are presented with more options, each of which has its advantages and disadvantages in terms of advancing normalisation, safety, cost, and quality assurance.[56]

A related issue is whether to plan specialist services for people with disabilities, or to modify generic services to offer specialist support when necessary. Within the normalisation approach the second option is preferable. Yet within the users' movement the first is seen as the way forward (see Chapter 3), as is the case with services for ethnic minorities.

8. Innovative policies of organisational change are often those which put existing resources to a new use, rather than focusing on the introduction of brand new resources. Closing down a service in order to use the staff and the resources for a new purpose, as exemplified in the ENCOR programme (see reference 18) when the organisation stopped delivering a direct service and moved into training, demonstrates one such instance.

In conclusion, the availability of opportunities for ordinary living, and the degree of control over their lives of people with disabilities has increased since the 1950s, but not systematically. It is as if some of this has been put into practice in spite of existing policies, rather than because of them. At the same time, a number of policies has been set out to achieve these objectives. Perhaps this is yet another example of a creative use of existing resources.

Policy-makers have been walking a tightrope in planning for normalisation, often not aiming at it, being pressurised by opposing factions, and genuinely grappling with the unknown. The complexity of the task cannot be overstated. While the majority did not live up to this challenge, some have risen to it and offer positive examples to all of us.

## References

1. Wolfe, B.L., *Impacts of Disability and Some Policy Implications* (Madison, Wis.: Institute for Research on Poverty, 1979); Townsend, P., *The Government Must Do Its Sums Better on Disability* (London: Disability Alliance, 1981).
2. Smith, M., *Disability in Great Britain* (London: OPCS, 1989).
3. Glennerster, H. (ed.) *The Future of the Welfare State: Remaking Social Policy* (London: Heinemann, 1983); Flora, P. and Heidenheimer, A.J. (eds), *The Development of Welfare States in Europe* (New Brunswick: Transaction Books, 1981).

4. Robinson, D. and Henry, S., *Self Help and Health: Mutual Aid for Modern Problems* (London: Robertson, 1977); Gartley, C., *Managing Incontinence* (London: Souvenir Books, 1989).
5. Andrain, C.F., *Social Policies in Western Industrial Societies* (Berkeley: Institute of International Studies, University of California, 1985).
6. Ward, L. 'Blinded by the Light', *Community Care*, 19 July 1990, pp. 18–19.
7. Hall, P., Land, H., Webb, A. and Parker, R., *Change, Choice and Conflict in Social Policy* (London: Heinemann, 1975).
8. Brown, P., *The Transfer of Care* (London: Routledge & Kegan Paul, 1985).
9. Tranchina, P. and Basaglia, F. (eds), *Autobiografia di'un Movimento, 1961–1979* (Ammistrazione Provinciale di Arezzo, 1979); Scull, A., *Decarceration* (Englewood Cliffs, NJ: Prentice-Hall, 1975).
10. Brost, M. and Johnson, T., *Getting to Know You* (Madison, Wis.: Wisconsin Coalition for Advocacy and New Concepts for the Handicapped Foundation, 1982).
11. Mount, B., Beeman, P. and Ducharme, G., *What Are We Learning About Circles of Support?* (Connecticut: Communitas, 1988).
12. Del Giudice, G., Evaristo, P. and Reali, M., 'How Can Mental Hospitals be Phased Out?' in Ramon, S. (ed.). *Psychiatry in Transition* (London: Pluto Press, 1988) pp. 199–207; Rotelli, F., 'Changing Psychiatric Services in Italy', ibid., pp. 182–90; De Nicola, P., Giacobbi, E. and Rogialli, S., 'Changing Professional Roles in the Italian Psychiatric System', ibid., pp. 235–42.
13. Mauri, D., *La Liberta E Terapeutica?* (Rome: Fletrinelli, 1984).
14. See Brown, P. in 7 above and: Reid, H. and Wiseman, A., *When the Talking Has to Stop* (London: MIND, 1986).
15. Brangwyn, G., 'Constructing a Crisis-focused Social Service', in Ramon, S. (ed.) *Psychiatry in Transition*, 11 above, pp. 49–59. For a different approach concerning alternatives to asylums see also: Del'Acqua, G. and Mezzina, R., 'Approaching Mental Distress', ibid., pp. 60–71.
16. Sain, F., Norcio, B. and Malannino, S. 'Compulsory Health Treatment: The Experience in Trieste from 1978 to 1988', in *For Mental Health: Practices, Research, Cultures in the Process of Innovation*, vol.4, Regional Centre for Mental Health Studies, Friuli-Venezia Giulia, 1990, pp. 137–52.
17. Wolfensberger, W., 'Social Role Valorisation: A Proposed New Term for the Principle of Normalisation', *Mental Retardation*, vol.21, no.6, 1983, pp. 234–9.
18. Stark, J.A., McGee. J.J. and Menolascino, F.J., *International Handbook of Community Services for the Mentally Retarded* (Hillsdale NJ: Lawrence Erlbaum, 1984).
19. Bank-Mikkelson, N.E., 'A Metropolitan Area in Denmark: Copenhagen', in Kugel, R. (ed.), *Changing Patterns of Residential Services for the Mentally Retarded* (Washington DC: President's Committee for the Mentally Retarded, 1969) pp. 241–52.

20. See 18 above, p. 113.
21. Brandon, D. and Towe, N. *Free to Choose: An Introduction to Service Brokerage* (London: Good Impressions, 1989).
22. Hennelly, R., 'Mental Health Resource Centres', in Ramon, S. (ed.), *Psychiatry in Transition*, see 9 above, pp. 208–18.
23. Cuvo, A.J. and Davis, P.K., 'Home Living for Developmentally Disabled Persons: Instructional Design and Evaluation', *Exceptional Education Quarterly*, vol.2, no.1, 1981, pp. 87–98; Flynn, M., 'Independent Living Arrangements for Adults Who Are Mentally Handicapped', in Malin, N. (ed.), *Community Care Reassessed* (London: Croom Helm, 1987) pp. 302–22; Rioux, M. and Crawford, C., *Choices: The Community Living Concept as a Way of Thinking* (Vancouver: Community Living Society, 1982).
24. Kay, A. and Legg, C., *Discharged to the Community: A Review of Housing and Support in London for People Leaving Psychiatric Care* (London: City University, 1985).
25. See 12 above.
26. Garety, P., 'Housing', in Lavender, A. and Holloway, F. (eds), *Community Care in Practice: Services for the Continuing Care Client* (London: Wiley, 1988) pp. 143–60.
27. Brazil, R. and Carle, N., 'An Ordinary Home Life', in Towell, D. (ed.), *An Ordinary Life in Practice* (London: King Edward's Hospital Fund for London, 1988) pp. 59–67.
28. Meyer, L.H. and Kishi, G.S., 'School Integration Strategies', in Lakin, K.C. and Bruininks, R.H. (eds), *Strategies for Achieving Community Integration of Developmentally Disabled Citizens* (Baltimore: Paul Brooks, 1985) pp. 231–52; OECD, *The Education of the Handicapped Adolescent: Integration of Handicapped Children in Italy* (Paris: OCED, 1979).
29. Salvi, E. and Cecchini, M., 'Children with Handicaps in Ordinary Schools', in Ramon, S. (ed.), Psychiatry in Transition, see 9 above, pp. 138–46.
30. Glendinning, C., *Unshared Care: Parents and Their Disabled Children* (London: Routledge & Kegan Paul, 1983); Lahousnia, Z., *The Meaning of Mental Handicap and Community Care: Moslem and Non-Moslem Parents' Perspectives*, unpublished Ph.D. thesis, the London School of Economics, 1989.
31. Warner, R., *Recovery from Schizophrenia* (London: Routledge & Kegan Paul, 1987).
32. Tudor, K., 'The Politics of Disability in Italy: La Lega per il Diritto al Lavoro degli Handicappati', *Critical Social Policy*, 1988, pp. 37–54.
33. Vox Employment Service, The Base Document and Committee Report, London Borough of Hillingdon, 1989.
34. Olshansky, S., 'Vocational Behaviour Through Normalisation', in Wolfensberger, W. (ed.), *Normalisation: The Principle of Normalisation in Human Services* (Toronto: National Institute for Medical Research, 1972) pp. 151–63; Di Mascio, A., 'La Riproduzione Sociale Dell'utenza', in Righetti, A. (ed.), *La Questione Psichiatrica* (Pordenone:

Centro Studie Salute Mentale, 1988) pp. 253–6; Sikking, M., *Co-ops with a Difference: Workers' Co-ops for People with Special Needs* (London: ICOM Co-publications, London, 1986).

35. Pilling, S., 'Work and the Continuing Care Client', in Lavender, A. and Holloway, F. (ed.), *Community Care in Practice*, see 20 above, pp. 187–205; Porterfield, J., 'Promoting Opportunities for Employment', in Towell, D. (ed.), *An Ordinary Life in Practice* (London: King's Fund Publications, 1988) pp. 80–9.

36. Sherman, P.S. and Porter, R., 'The Colorado Consumer Case-manager Aide Program', *Journal of Psychosocial Rehabilitation*, 1990.

37. Sainsbury, S., *Deaf Worlds* (London: Hutchinson, 1986).

38. Tihanyi, P., *Volunteers: Why They Come and Why They Stay. A Study of the Motives and Rewards of Volunteers Working in a Jewish Day Centre*, M.A. thesis, Centre for the Management of Voluntary Organisations, Brunel University, 1988.

39. PSSRU, *Care in the Community*, Summer 1985, the University of Kent, Canterbury.

40. See 30 above.

41. Cox, G.B., 'Programme Evaluation', in Austin, M.J. and Hershey, W.E. (eds), *Handbook on Mental Health Administration* (San Francisco: Jossey Bass, 1982).

42. Wolfensberger, W. and Glenn, L., *PASS–Programme Analysis of Service Systems*, 3rd edn (Toronto, Institute of Mental Retardation, 1975); Wolfensberger, W. and Thomas, S., *PASSING–Programme Analysis of Service Systems' Implementation of Normalisation Goals* (Toronto: National Institute on Mental Retardation, 1983).

43. Tyne, A., 'Shaping Community Services: The Impact of an Idea', in Malin, N. (ed.), *Community Care Reassessed* (London: Croom Helm, pp. 80–96).

44. See 18 above.

45. Sainsbury, S., *Regulating Residential Care* (Aldershot: Avebury, 1989); The Royal College of Psychiatrists, *Mental Health Services in Britain: The Way Ahead* (London: Gaskell, 1986) pp. 102–10.

46. Korman, N. and Glennerster, H., *Hospital Closure* (Milton Keynes: Open University Press, 1990) pp. 144–57.

47. See 18 above, pp. 206–17.

48. Shiell, A. and Wright, K., 'The Economic Costs', in Alaszewski, A. and Ong, B.N. (eds), *Normalisation in Practice* (London: Tavistock, 1990) pp. 249–66.

49. Beecham, J. and Knapp, M., 'The Costs of Psychiatric Reprovision: Community Care for Former Long-stay Hospital Residents', Discussion Paper 653, Personal Social Services Research Unit, University of Kent, January 1990.

50. Challis, L. (ed.), *Joint Approaches to Social Policy* (Cambridge: Cambridge University Press, 1988).

51. Mahoney, J., 'Finance and Government Policy', in Lavender, A. and Holloway, F. (eds), *Community Care in Practice*.

52. Capitman, J.A., Haskins, B. and Bernstein, J., 'Case Management Approaches in Coordinated Community-oriented Long-term Care Demonstrations', *The Gerontologist*, vol.26, no.4, 1986; Hunter, D.J. (ed.), *Bridging the Gap: Case Management and Advocacy for People with Physical Handicaps* (London: King's Fund Publications, 1988); Clifford, P. and Craig, T., *Case Management Systems for Long-term Mentally Ill* (London: National Unit for Psychiatric Research and Development, 1989); Beardshaw, V. and Towell, D., *Assessment and Care Management: Implications for the Implementation of 'Caring for People'* (London: King's Fund Institute, 1990). For the best American example of case management see: Test, M.A., 'The Training in Community Living Model: Delivering Treatment and Rehabilitation Services Through a Continuous Treatment Team', in Liberman, R.P. (ed.), *Rehabilitation of the Seriously Mentally Ill* (New York: Plenum, 1987).

53. Salisbury, B., Dickey, J. and Crawford, C., *Service Brokerage: Individual Empowerment and Social Service Accountability* (Downsview, Ontario: The G. Allan Roeher Institute, 1987).

54. See 45 above.

55. Bachrach, L., *The Lessons Learnt from Demonstration Projects in the US*, paper given at the Good Practices in Mental Health study day on British Mental Health Demonstration Projects, London, 10 November 1988; Georgiades, N.J. and Phillimore, L., 'The Myth of the Hero-Innovator and Alternative Strategies for Organisational Change', in Kiernan, C.C. and Woodford, E.P. (eds), *Behaviour Modification with the Severely Retarded* (Amsterdam: Elsevier, Associated Scientific Publishers, 1975); Renshaw, J., 'The Future of Demonstration Projects, New Directions', *Good Practices in Mental Health*, Summer 1989, pp. 2–3.

56. Blunden, R., 'Safeguarding Quality', in Towell, D. (ed.), *An Ordinary Life in Practice* (London: King Edward's Hospital Fund for London) pp. 106–16.

# Name Index

# Subject Index